Wonderful ways to prepare

BISCUITS & COOKIES

by JO ANN SHIRLEY

TITLES AVAILABLE

Wonderful Ways to Prepare
HORS D'OEUVRES & FIRST COURSES
SOUPS
MEAT
FISH & SEAFOOD
STEWS & CASSEROLES
SALADS
DESSERTS
CAKES & COOKIES
BARBECUES
ITALIAN FOOD
CHINESE DISHES
CROCKERY POT DISHES
FOOD FOR FREEZING
PRESERVES
VEGETARIAN DISHES
CALORIE CONTROLLED DISHES
CHEESECAKES
COCKTAILS & MIXED DRINKS
CHICKEN
MEALS IN A WOK
MICROWAVE DISHES
EGGS
PRESSURE COOKER DISHES
ASIAN MEALS
BISCUITS AND COOKIES
CAKES AND SWEETS
CREPES & PANCAKES
BLENDER & MIXER DISHES
FONDUES

Wonderful ways to prepare

BISCUITS & COOKIES

PUBLISHED BY
PLAYMORE INC. New York, USA
AND WALDMAN PUBLISHING CORP. New York, USA

AYERS & JAMES
CROWS NEST AUSTRALIA

FIRST PUBLISHED 1983

PUBLISHED BY
PLAYMORE INC. New York, USA
AND WALDMAN PUBLISHING CORP. New York, USA

PUBLISHED IN AUSTRALIA
BY AYERS & JAMES
CROWS NEST. AUSTRALIA

COPYRIGHT 1983
AYERS.& JAMES PTY. LTD.
5 ALEXANDER STREET
CROWS NEST N.S.W. AUSTRALIA

PRINTED IN CANADA

ISBN 0 86908-236 1

OVEN TEMPERATURE GUIDE

Description	Gas		Electric		Mark
	C	F	C	F	
Cool	100	200	110	225	¼
Very Slow	120	250	120	250	½
Slow	150	300	150	300	1-2
Moderately slow	160	325	170	340	3
Moderate	180	350	200	400	4
Moderately hot	190	375	220	425	5-6
Hot	200	400	230	450	6-7
Very hot	230	450	250	475	8-9

LIQUID MEASURES

IMPERIAL	METRIC
1 teaspoon	5 ml
1 tablespoon	20 ml
2 fluid ounces (¼ cup)	62.5 ml
4 fluid ounces (½ cup)	125 ml
8 fluid ounces (1 cup)	250 ml
1 pint (16 ounces — 2 cups)*	500 ml

* (The imperial pint is equal to 20 fluid ounces.)

SOLID MEASURES

AVOIRDUPOIS	METRIC
1 ounce	30 g
4 ounces (¼ lb)	125 g
8 ounces (½ lb)	250 g
12 ounces (¾ lb)	375 g
16 ounces (1 lb)	500 g
24 ounces (1½ lb)	750 g
32 ounces (2 lb)	1000 g (1 kg)

CUP AND SPOON REPLACEMENTS FOR OUNCES

INGREDIENT	½ oz	1 oz	2 oz	3 oz	4 oz	5 oz	6 oz	7 oz	8 oz
Almonds, ground	2 T	¼ C	½ C	¾ C	1¼ C	1⅓ C	1⅔ C	2 C	2¼ C
slivered	6 t	¼ C	½ C	¾ C	1 C	1⅓ C	1⅔ C	2 C	2¼ C
whole	2 T	¼ C	⅓ C	½ C	¾ C	1 C	1¼ C	1⅓ C	1½ C
Apples, dried whole	3 T	½ C	1 C	1⅓ C	2 C	2⅓ C	2¾ C	3⅓ C	3¾ C
Apricots, chopped	2 T	¼ C	½ C	¾ C	1 C	1¼ C	1½ C	1¾ C	2 C
whole	2 T	3 T	½ C	⅔ C	1 C	1¼ C	1⅓ C	1½ C	1¾ C
Arrowroot	1 T	2 T	⅓ C	½ C	⅔ C	¾ C	1 C	1¼ C	1⅓ C
Baking Powder	1 T	2 T	⅓ C	½ C	⅔ C	¾ C	1 C	1 C	1¼ C
Baking Soda	1 T	2 T	⅓ C	½ C	⅔ C	¾ C	1 C	1 C	1¼ C
Barley	1 T	2 T	¼ C	½ C	⅔ C	¾ C	1 C	1 C	1¼ C
Breadcrumbs, dry	2 T	¼ C	½ C	¾ C	1 C	1¼ C	1½ C	1¾ C	2 C
soft	¼ C	½ C	1 C	1½ C	2 C	2½ C	3 C	3⅔ C	4¼ C
Biscuit Crumbs	2 T	¼ C	½ C	¾ C	1¼ C	1⅓ C	1⅔ C	2 C	2¼ C
Butter	3 t	6 t	¼ C	⅓ C	½ C	⅔ C	¾ C	1 C	1 C
Cheese, grated, lightly packed,									
natural cheddar	6 t	¼ C	½ C	¾ C	1 C	1¼ C	1½ C	1¾ C	2 C
Processed cheddar	5 t	2 T	⅓ C	⅔ C	¾ C	1 C	1¼ C	1½ C	1⅔ C
Parmesan, Romano	6 t	¼ C	½ C	¾ C	1 C	1⅓ C	1⅔ C	2 C	2¼ C
Cherries, candied, chopped	1 T	2 T	⅓ C	½ C	¾ C	1 C	1 C	1⅓ C	1½ C
whole	1 T	2 T	⅓ C	½ C	⅔ C	¾ C	1 C	1¼ C	1⅓ C
Cocoa	2 T	¼ C	½ C	¾ C	1¼ C	1⅓ C	1⅔ C	2 C	2¼ C
Coconut, desiccated	2 T	⅓ C	⅔ C	1 C	1⅓ C	1⅔ C	2 C	2⅓ C	2⅔ C
shredded	⅓ C	⅔ C	1¼ C	1¾ C	2½ C	3 C	3⅔ C	4⅓ C	5 C
Cornstarch	6 t	3 T	½ C	⅔ C	1 C	1¼ C	1½ C	1⅔ C	2 C
Corn Syrup	2 t	1 T	2 T	¼ C	⅓ C	½ C	½ C	⅔ C	⅔ C
Coffee, ground	2 T	⅓ C	⅔ C	1 C	1⅓ C	1⅔ C	2 C	2⅓ C	2⅔ C
instant	3 T	½ C	1 C	1⅓ C	1¾ C	2¼ C	2⅔ C	3 C	3½ C
Cornflakes	½ C	1 C	2 C	3 C	4¼ C	5¼ C	6¼ C	7⅓ C	8⅓ C
Cream of Tartar	1 T	2 T	⅓ C	½ C	⅔ C	¾ C	1 C	1 C	1¼ C
Currants	1 T	2 T	⅓ C	⅔ C	¾ C	1 C	1¼ C	1½ C	1⅔ C
Custard Powder	6 t	3 T	½ C	⅔ C	1 C	1¼ C	1½ C	1⅔ C	2 C
Dates, chopped	1 T	2 T	⅓ C	⅔ C	¾ C	1 C	1¼ C	1½ C	1⅔ C
whole, pitted	1 T	2 T	⅓ C	½ C	¾ C	1 C	1¼ C	1⅓ C	1½ C
Figs, chopped	1 T	2 T	⅓ C	½ C	¾ C	1 C	1 C	1⅓ C	1½ C
Flour, all-purpose or cake	6 t	¼ C	½ C	¾ C	1 C	1¼ C	1½ C	1¾ C	2 C
wholemeal	6 t	3 T	½ C	⅔ C	1 C	1¼ C	1⅓ C	1⅔ C	1¾ C
Fruit, mixed	1 T	2 T	⅓ C	½ C	¾ C	1 C	1¼ C	1⅓ C	1½ C
Gelatine	5 t	2 T	⅓ C	½ C	¾ C	1 C	1 C	1¼ C	1½ C
Ginger, crystallised pieces	1 T	2 T	⅓ C	½ C	¾ C	1 C	1¼ C	1⅓ C	1½ C
ground	6 t	⅓ C	½ C	¾ C	1¼ C	1½ C	1¾ C	2 C	2¼ C
preserved, heavy syrup	1 T	2 T	⅓ C	½ C	⅔ C	¾ C	1 C	1 C	1¼ C
Glucose, liquid	2 t	1 T	2 T	¼ C	⅓ C	½ C	½ C	⅔ C	⅔ C
Haricot Beans	1 T	2 T	⅓ C	½ C	⅔ C	¾ C	1 C	1 C	1¼ C

In this table, t represents teaspoonful, T represents tablespoonful and C represents cupful.

CUP AND SPOON REPLACEMENTS FOR OUNCES (Cont.)

INGREDIENT	½ oz	1 oz	2 oz	3 oz	4 oz	5 oz	6 oz	7 oz	8 oz
Honey	2 t	1 T	2 T	¼ C	⅓ C	½ C	½ C	⅔ C	⅔ C
Jam	2 t	1 T	2 T	¼ C	⅓ C	½ C	½ C	⅔ C	¾ C
Lentils	1 T	2 T	⅓ C	½ C	⅔ C	¾ C	1 C	1 C	1¼ C
Macaroni (see pasta)									
Milk Powder, full cream	2 T	¼ C	½ C	¾ C	1¼ C	1⅓ C	1⅔ C	2 C	2¼ C
non fat	2 T	⅓ C	¾ C	1¼ C	1½ C	2 C	2⅓ C	2¾ C	3¼ C
Nutmeg	6 t	3 T	½ C	⅔ C	¾ C	1 C	1¼ C	1½ C	1⅔ C
Nuts, chopped	6 t	¼ C	½ C	¾ C	1 C	1¼ C	1½ C	1¾ C	2 C
Oatmeal	1 T	2 T	½ C	⅔ C	¾ C	1 C	1¼ C	1½ C	1⅔ C
Olives, whole	1 T	2 T	⅓ C	⅔ C	¾ C	1 C	1¼ C	1½ C	1⅔ C
sliced	1 T	2 T	⅓ C	⅔ C	¾ C	1 C	1¼ C	1½ C	1⅔ C
Pasta, short (e.g. macaroni)	1 T	2 T	⅓ C	⅔ C	¾ C	1 C	1¼ C	1½ C	1⅔ C
Peaches, dried & whole	1 T	2 T	⅓ C	⅔ C	¾ C	1 C	1¼ C	1½ C	1⅔ C
chopped	6 t	¼ C	½ C	¾ C	1 C	1¼ C	1½ C	1¾ C	2 C
Peanuts, shelled, raw, whole	1 T	2 T	⅓ C	½ C	¾ C	1 C	1¼ C	1⅓ C	1½ C
roasted	1 T	2 T	⅓ C	⅔ C	¾ C	1 C	1¼ C	1½ C	1⅔ C
Peanut Butter	3 t	6 t	3 T	⅓ C	½ C	½ C	⅔ C	¾ C	1 C
Peas, split	1 T	2 T	⅓ C	½ C	⅔ C	¾ C	1 C	1 C	1¼ C
Peel, mixed	1 T	2 T	⅓ C	½ C	¾ C	1 C	1 C	1¼ C	1½ C
Potato, powder	1 T	2 T	¼ C	⅓ C	½ C	⅔ C	¾ C	1 C	1¼ C
flakes	¼ C	½ C	1 C	1⅓ C	2 C	2⅓ C	2¾ C	3⅓ C	3¾ C
Prunes, chopped	1 T	2 T	⅓ C	½ C	⅔ C	¾ C	1 C	1¼ C	1⅓ C
whole pitted	1 T	2 T	⅓ C	½ C	⅔ C	¾ C	1 C	1 C	1¼ C
Raisins	2 T	¼ C	⅓ C	½ C	¾ C	1 C	1 C	1⅓ C	1½ C
Rice, short grain, raw	1 T	2 T	¼ C	½ C	⅔ C	¾ C	1 C	1 C	1¼ C
long grain, raw	1 T	2 T	⅓ C	½ C	¾ C	1 C	1¼ C	1⅓ C	1½ C
Rice Bubbles	⅔ C	1¼ C	2½ C	3⅔ C	5 C	6¼ C	7½ C	8¾ C	10 C
Rolled Oats	2 T	⅓ C	⅔ C	1 C	1⅓ C	1¾ C	2 C	2½ C	2¾ C
Sago	2 T	¼ C	⅓ C	½ C	¾ C	1 C	1 C	1¼ C	1½ C
Salt, common	3 t	6 t	¼ C	⅓ C	½ C	⅔ C	¾ C	1 C	1 C
Semolina	1 T	2 T	⅓ C	½ C	¾ C	1 C	1 C	1⅓ C	1½ C
Spices	6 t	3 T	¼ C	⅓ C	½ C	½ C	⅔ C	¾ C	1 C
Sugar, plain	3 t	6 t	¼ C	⅓ C	½ C	⅔ C	¾ C	1 C	1 C
confectioners'	1 T	2 T	⅓ C	½ C	¾ C	1 C	1 C	1¼ C	1½ C
moist brown	1 T	2 T	⅓ C	½ C	¾ C	1 C	1 C	1⅓ C	1½ C
Tapioca	1 T	2 T	⅓ C	½ C	⅔ C	¾ C	1 C	1¼ C	1⅓ C
Treacle	2 t	1 T	2 T	¼ C	⅓ C	½ C	½ C	⅔ C	⅔ C
Walnuts, chopped	2 T	¼ C	½ C	¾ C	1 C	1¼ C	1½ C	1¾ C	2 C
halved	2 T	⅓ C	⅔ C	1 C	1¼ C	1½ C	1¾ C	2¼ C	2½ C
Yeast, dried	6 t	3 T	½ C	⅔ C	1 C	1¼ C	1⅓ C	1⅔ C	1¾ C
compressed	3 t	6 t	3 T	⅓ C	½ C	½ C	⅔ C	¾ C	1 C

In this table, t represents teaspoonful, T represents tablespoonful and C represents cupful.

Biscuits and Cookies

Bird's Nest Cookies

1 cup (250 g) butter
½ cup sugar
¼ teaspoon salt
2 egg yolks
1½ teaspoons vanilla

2 cups all-purpose flour
1 egg white
1 cup chopped nuts
chocolate bits

1. Cream together the butter and sugar until light and fluffy.
2. Add the salt, egg yolks and vanilla and beat well.
3. Sift the flour and add to the mixture.
4. Shape into small balls.
5. Beat the egg white until foamy and dip the balls first into the egg whites and then roll in the chopped nuts.
6. Place on a cookie sheet about one inch (2½ cm) apart. Make a depression in the center of each cookie.
7. Bake in a 375°F (190°C) oven for about 15 minutes. Remove from the oven and while the cookies are still warm, press chocolate bits in the center.

Makes about 3 dozen.

Butter Almond Cookies

¾ cup (185 g) butter
¼ cup sugar
½ teaspoon almond extract
2 cups all-purpose flour
⅛ teaspoon salt

1 egg white, slightly beaten
2 tablespoons sugar
¼ teaspoon cinnamon
½ cup finely chopped blanched almonds

1. Cream together the butter and sugar until light and fluffy.
2. Add the almond extract.
3. Sift the flour with the salt and add to the mixture. Blend thoroughly. Chill for at least an hour.
4. Roll out on a floured board to a thickness of ¼ inch (6 mm). Cut into rounds and place on a buttered cookie sheet.
5. Brush with the egg white.
6. Mix together the sugar, cinnamon and almonds and sprinkle on the cookies.
7. Bake in a 350°F (180°C) oven for about ten minutes.

Makes about 3 dozen.

Nut Ball Cookies

½ cup (125 g) butter
¼ cup sugar
1 egg yolk
1 tablespoon grated orange rind
1½ teaspoons grated lemon rind

1 tablespoon lemon juice
1 teaspoon vanilla
1 cup cake flour
1 egg white, slightly beaten
¾ cup finely chopped nuts

1. Cream together the butter and sugar until light and fluffy.
2. Add the egg yolk, grated rinds, lemon juice and vanilla and beat well.
3. Sift the flour and add to the mixture. Chill for at least an hour.
4. Shape into small balls. Dip in the slightly beaten egg white and roll in the nuts. Place on a buttered cookie sheet.
5. Bake in a 375°F (190°C) oven for about 15 minutes.

Makes about 2 dozen.

Chocolate Nut Shortbread

1 cup (250 g) butter
2 oz (60 g) cooking chocolate,
   melted
1½ cups confectioners' sugar
2¼ cups all-purpose flour
⅔ cup chopped walnuts

1. Cream the butter and stir in the cooled chocolate.
2. Add the sugar and beat well.
3. Sift the flour and stir into the mixture with the nuts.
4. Shape into a roll about 2 inches (5 cm) in diameter. Wrap in wax paper and chill for several hours.
5. Cut into ¼-inch (5-mm) slices and place on a lightly buttered cookie sheet.
6. Bake in a 325°F (160°C) oven for about 20 minutes.

Makes about 3 dozen.

Lemon Shortbread Cookies

4 cups all-purpose flour
¼ teaspoon salt
1 cup brown sugar
1¼ tablespoons grated lemon
   rind

2 cups (500 g) butter
1 egg white
glacé cherries

1. Sift the flour with the salt and mix with the sugar and lemon rind.
2. Add the butter and mix to a smooth dough. Chill for an hour.
3. Roll out on a floured board to a thickness of ½ inch (one cm). Cut out with a floured cookie cutter.
4. Brush with the egg white and decorate with glacé cherries. Place on a cookie sheet.
5. Bake in a 350°F (180°C) oven for 15 minutes.

Makes about 3 dozen.

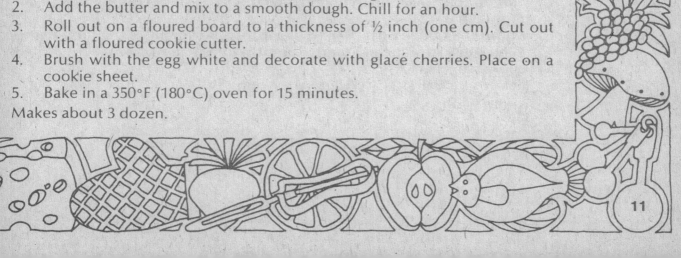

Walnut Crispies

1 cup (250 g) butter
2½ cups brown sugar
2 eggs
2½ cups all-purpose flour

¼ teaspoon salt
½ teaspoon baking soda
1 cup chopped walnuts

1. Cream together the butter and sugar until light and fluffy.
2. Add the eggs one at a time beating well after each addition.
3. Sift together the flour, salt and baking soda and add to the creamed mixture.
4. Stir in the walnuts blending thoroughly.
5. Drop by the spoonful onto a buttered cookie sheet.
6. Bake in a 350°F (180°C) oven for about 15 minutes.

Makes about 5 dozen.

Lemon Wafers

2 cups all-purpose flour
1½ teaspoons baking powder
½ teaspoon ground ginger
⅛ teaspoon salt
¼ cup (65 g) butter

½ cup sugar
2 teaspoons grated lemon rind
2 tablespoons lemon juice
2 tablespoons light corn syrup

1. Sift together the flour, baking powder, ginger and salt.
2. Add the butter and mix well.
3. Stir in the sugar, lemon rind, lemon juice and corn syrup. Blend thoroughly.
4. Knead the dough on a floured board for a few minutes then roll out to a thickness of ⅛ inch (3 mm). Cut into rounds and place on a buttered cookie sheet.
5. Bake in a 400°F (200°C) oven for ten minutes.

Makes about 4 dozen.

Orange Thins

1 cup (250 g) butter
1¼ cups sugar
2 tablespoons grated orange rind
1 egg
4 cups all-purpose flour

1 teaspoon cinnamon
½ teaspoon crushed cardamom seed
½ cup ground nuts
¼ cup (65 ml) orange juice
¾ teaspoon salt

1. Cream together the butter and sugar until light and fluffy.
2. Add the orange rind and egg and beat well.
3. Sift together the flour, salt and cinnamon and add to the mixture.
4. Add the crushed cardamom, nuts and orange juice and blend thoroughly.
5. Roll out on a floured board to a thickness of ¼ inch (5 mm). Cut into shapes desired and place on a buttered cookie sheet.
6. Bake in a 425°F (220°C) oven for about five minutes.

Makes about 8 dozen.

Digestive Cookies

1½ cups all-purpose flour
2 teaspoons baking powder
½ teaspoon salt
¼ cup ground oats

¼ cup sugar
3 tablespoons (60 g) lard
milk

1. Sift together the flour, baking powder and salt.
2. Add the oats and sugar and mix well.
3. Rub in the lard.
4. Add enough milk to form a firm dough.
5. Knead on a floured board. Roll out thinly and prick with a fork. Cut into rounds and place on a buttered cookie sheet.
6. Bake in a 400°F (200°C) oven for about 15 minutes.

Makes about 2 dozen.

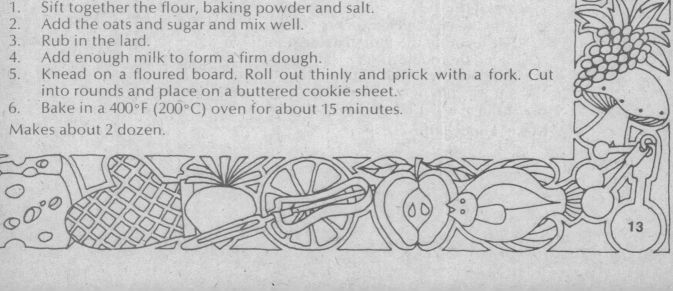

Honey-Spice Cookies

½ cup (125 g) butter
½ cup honey
1 egg
1 teaspoon baking powder

1 cup wholemeal flour
1 cup all-purpose flour
2 teaspoons mixed spice

1. Thoroughly beat together the butter and honey.
2. Add the egg and beat well.
3. Sift together the baking powder, wholemeal flour, all-purpose flour and mixed spice. Add to the honey mixture and blend well. Chill for at least an hour.
4. Roll out on a floured board to a thickness of ¼ inch (5 mm). Cut into rounds and place on a buttered cookie sheet.
5. Bake in a 450°F (230°C) oven for about ten minutes.

Makes about 3 dozen.

Strawberry Cookies

⅓ cup instant strawberry flavored
    beverage mix
⅔ cup sugar
⅔ cup (165 g) butter
1 egg

1 tablespoon lemon juice
2 cups all-purpose flour
2 teaspoons baking powder
½ teaspoon salt

1. Cream together the strawberry flavored mix, sugar and butter until light and fluffy.
2. Add the egg and lemon juice and beat well.
3. Sift together the flour, baking powder and salt and add to the mixture. Blend thoroughly.
4. Roll out on a floured board to a thickness of about ¼ inch (5 mm). Cut into shapes desired and place on a cookie sheet.
5. Bake in a 350°F (180°C) oven for about ten minutes.

Makes about 3 dozen.

Island Cookies

2⅓ cups all-purpose flour	½ cup peanut butter
1 teaspoon baking powder	1 cup sugar
½ teaspoon salt	1 egg
⅓ cup (85 g) butter	1 cup crushed pineapple

1. Sift together the flour, baking powder and salt. Set aside.
2. Cream together the butter, peanut butter and sugar until light and fluffy.
3. Add the egg and beat well.
4. Stir in the crushed pineapple.
5. Gradually add the sifted dry ingredients. Mix thoroughly.
6. Form into oblong shapes and place on a buttered cookie sheet.
7. Bake in a 375°F (190°C) oven for about ten minutes.

Makes about 4 dozen.

Rock Cakes

½ cup (125 g) butter	1 teaspoon baking powder
½ cup sugar	⅛ teaspoon salt
3 eggs	1 cup raisins
1¼ teaspoons vanilla	½ cup chopped glacé cherries
2 cups all-purpose flour	½ cup chopped walnuts

1. Cream together the butter and sugar until light and fluffy.
2. Add the eggs one at a time beating well after each addition.
3. Add the vanilla.
4. Sift together the flour, baking powder and salt and add to the mixture.
5. Stir in the raisins, cherries and walnuts. Blend thoroughly.
6. Drop by the spoonful onto a buttered cookie sheet.
7. Bake in a 350°F (180°C) oven for about 12 minutes.

Makes about 3 dozen.

Banana Oatmeal Cookies

1½ cups all-purpose flour
1 teaspoon baking powder
½ teaspoon baking soda
⅛ teaspoon salt
1 teaspoon cinnamon
¼ teaspoon nutmeg

1 cup sugar
⅔ cup (165 g) butter
2 eggs
1 cup mashed bananas
1½ cups rolled oats

1. Sift together the flour, baking powder, baking soda, salt, cinnamon, nutmeg and sugar.
2. Add the butter, eggs and half the mashed bananas. Beat until smooth and creamy.
3. Fold in the rest of the bananas and the rolled oats.
4. Drop by the spoonful onto a buttered cookie sheet.
5. Bake in a 375°F (190°C) oven for about 15 minutes.

Makes about 4 dozen.

Almond Crescents

2 cups (500 g) butter
2¼ cups sugar
4 eggs
1 lb (500 g) ground almonds
1½ tablespoons grated lemon
   rind

4 cups all-purpose flour
2 egg whites
¼ cup sugar
1 cup chopped blanched
   almonds

1. Cream together the butter and sugar until light and fluffy.
2. Add the eggs one at a time beating well after each addition.
3. Stir in the ground nuts, grated lemon rind and flour. Blend thoroughly. Chill for about an hour.
4. Roll out to a thickness of ¼ inch (5 mm) on a floured board. Cut into crescent shapes. Place on a buttered cookie sheet.
5. Mix together the egg whites, sugar and chopped almonds. Brush onto the crescents and set aside for one hour.
6. Bake in a 375°F (190°C) oven for about 12 minutes.

Makes about 6 dozen.

Christmas Cookies

½ cup finely chopped almonds
¾ cup (185 g) butter
½ cup brown sugar
¼ teaspoon nutmeg
¼ teaspoon ginger
¼ teaspoon ground cloves
1½ teaspoons cinnamon

2 tablespoons milk
2 cups all-purpose flour
1½ teaspoons baking powder
¼ teaspoon salt
¼ cup candied orange and lemon peel

1. Mix together the almonds, butter, sugar, spices and milk.
2. Sift the flour with the baking powder and salt and add to the mixture.
3. Stir in the peel and chill for at least an hour.
4. Roll the dough out on a floured board to a thickness of ¼ inch (5 mm). Cut into shapes desired. Place on a buttered cookie sheet.
5. Bake in a 375°F (190°C) oven for about seven minutes.

Makes about 3 dozen.

Mother's Special Cookies

3 cups cake flour
3 tablespoons sugar
⅛ teaspoon salt
3 egg yolks
¼ cup (65 ml) milk

½ lb (250 g) chopped walnuts
1 cup sugar
2 teaspoons cinnamon
cream

1. Sift together the flour, sugar and salt.
2. Add the egg yolks one at a time beating well after each addition.
3. Stir in the milk blending thoroughly. Chill for several hours.
4. Roll out on a floured board to a thickness of ⅛ inch (3 mm).
5. Mix together the walnuts, sugar, cinnamon, and enough cream to make a paste.
6. Spread the walnut mixture on the dough and roll up tightly. Cut into ¼ inch (5 mm) slices and place on a buttered cookie sheet.
7. Bake in a 375°F (190°C) oven for about ten minutes or until golden brown.

Makes about 3 dozen.

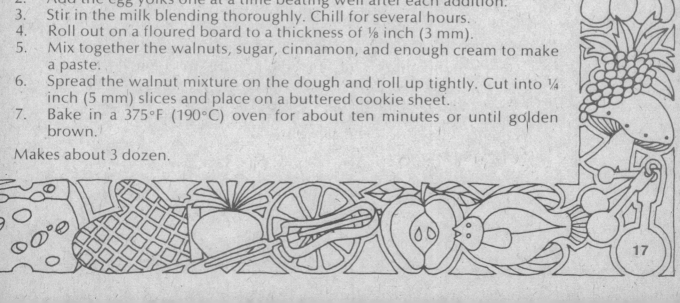

Nutmeg Butterballs

1 cup (250 g) butter
½ cup sugar
1½ teaspoons vanilla
2 cups all-purpose flour
⅛ teaspoon salt

1½ cups coarsely ground
  almonds
½ cup confectioners' sugar
2½ teaspoons nutmeg

1. Cream together the butter and sugar until light and fluffy.
2. Add the vanilla and mix well.
3. Sift together the flour and salt and add to the mixture with the almonds.
4. Shape into small balls and chill for at least an hour.
5. Place on a buttered cookie sheet and bake in a 300°F (150°C) oven for about 20 minutes.
6. Mix together the confectioners' sugar and nutmeg and while the cookies are still warm, roll them in the mixture.

Makes about 5 dozen.

Rice Shortbread

2½ cups all-purpose flour
1 cup rice flour
⅓ cup sugar
1 cup (250 g) butter (room
  temperature)
confectioners' sugar

1. Sift together the all-purpose flour, rice flour and sugar four times.
2. Cut the butter into the dry ingredients until well-blended.
3. Pat with your hands into a rectangle about ¾ inch (2 cm) thick. Cut into shapes desired and place on a cookie sheet.
4. Bake in a 325°F (160°C) oven for about 15 minutes. Sprinkle with confectioners' sugar and allow to cool.

Makes about 3 dozen.

Date Kisses

2 egg whites
¾ cup confectioners' sugar
1 cup ground nuts
1 cup finely chopped dates

1. Beat the egg whites until stiff.
2. Slowly add the sugar while continuing to beat.
3. Mix together the nuts and dates and add to the egg white mixture.
4. Drop by the spoonful onto a buttered cookie sheet.
5. Bake in a 325°F (160°C) oven for about eight minutes. Remove from the cookie sheet immediately after taking out of the oven.

Makes about 3 dozen.

Finnish Cookies

1 cup (250 g) butter	all-purpose flour
1⅓ cups confectioners' sugar	1 egg white
2 hard-boiled eggs	ground almonds
1 egg	cinnamon
¾ teaspoon vanilla	sugar

1. Cream together the butter and sugar until light and fluffy.
2. Chop the hard-boiled eggs then press through a sieve. Add to the creamed mixture.
3. Beat in the egg and vanilla.
4. Add just enough flour to form a soft dough.
5. Shape into small balls.
6. Flatten slightly and dip in lightly beaten egg white. Place on a buttered cookie sheet.
7. Make a mixture of almonds, cinnamon and sugar and sprinkle on the cookies.
8. Bake in a 375°F (190°C) oven for about ten minutes or until a pale golden color.

Makes about 6 dozen.

Lebkuchen

2 cups sugar
5 eggs (medium size)
1½ tablespoons grated lemon rind
1 lb (500 g) ground almonds
¼ (125 g) candied orange and lemon peel, finely chopped

1½ teaspoons nutmeg
1¼ teaspoons cinnamon
½ teaspoon ground cloves

Icing:
1 cup confectioners' sugar
2½ tablespoons lemon juice

1. Beat together the sugar, eggs and grated lemon rind with an electric mixer for 15 minutes.
2. Add the ground almonds, peel, nutmeg, cinnamon and cloves mixing by a hand. Mix to a stiff dough.
3. Drop by the spoonful onto a buttered cookie sheet about 2 inches (5 cm) apart.
4. Bake in a 350°F (180°C) oven for about ten minutes or until a pale golden color.
5. Make the icing by mixing together the sugar and lemon juice.
6. When the cookies are cool, spread on the icing.

Makes about 8 dozen.

Corn Meal Wafers

1 cup (250 g) butter
1 cup confectioners' sugar
½ cup corn meal
1 egg, separated
2 cups all-purpose flour
glacé cherries

1. Cream together the butter and sugar until light and fluffy.
2. Add the corn meal and mix thoroughly.
3. Add the egg yolk and beat well.
4. Beat the egg white until stiff and add to the mixture.
5. Sift the flour and gently stir in.
6. Drop by the spoonful onto a buttered cookie sheet.
7. Bake in a 350°F (180°C) oven for about ten minutes. Put a cherry on each cookie as soon as you remove them from the oven.

Makes about 4 dozen.

Sherry Balls

3 cups cake crumbs	½ cup (125 ml) sweet sherry
3 teaspoons corn syrup	1 cup chopped dates
1½ tablespoons cocoa	2 tablespoons chopped raisins
1 cup confectioners' sugar	1¼ teaspoons vanilla
¼ teaspoon cinnamon	confectioners' sugar

1. Mix together the cake crumbs, corn syrup, cocoa, sugar, cinnamon, sweet sherry, dates, raisins and vanilla.
2. Shape into small balls and roll in confectioners' sugar.
3. Set aside for about ½ hour before serving.

Makes about 3 dozen.

Victorian Tarts

½ cup sugar	⅛ teaspoon salt
1 cup (250 g) butter	½ teaspoon baking powder
2 egg yolks	2 cups all-purpose flour
1 teaspoon vanilla	jam

1. Cream together the sugar and butter until smooth.
2. Add the egg yolks one at a time beating well after each addition.
3. Stir in the vanilla.
4. Sift together the salt, baking powder and flour and add to the mixture. Blend thoroughly.
5. Roll out the dough on a floured board to a thickness of about ¼ inch (5 mm). Cut half the dough with a round cookie cutter and the other half with a doughnut cutter the same size. Place on a buttered cookie sheet.
6. Bake in a 350°F (180°C) oven for about eight minutes. When the cookies are cool, spread the rounds with jam and put the ones with holes on top. Put an extra dollop of jam in the holes. Sprinkle with confectioners' sugar if desired.

Makes about 18.

Tom Thumbs

1 cup (250 g) butter
½ cup brown sugar
2 cups all-purpose flour
2 eggs, separated
ground nuts
jam

1. Cream together the butter and sugar until light and fluffy.
2. Add the egg yolks one at a time beating well after each addition.
3. Stir in the flour blending thoroughly.
4. Shape the dough into small balls.
5. Beat the egg whites until frothy.
6. Dip the balls first into the egg whites, then roll in the ground nuts. Place on a cookie sheet.
7. Make a depression with your thumb in each ball.
8. Bake in a 350°F (180°C) oven for about 15 minutes.
9. Fill each depression with jam when slightly cooled.

Makes about 3 dozen.

Sour Cream Cookies

½ cup (125 g) butter
1½ cups sugar
3 eggs, beaten
1 cup (250 g) sour cream
1 teaspoon grated lemon rind

1 teaspoon baking soda
1 teaspoon lemon flavoring
1 teaspoon vanilla
all-purpose flour

1. Cream together the butter and sugar until light and fluffy.
2. Add the eggs and beat well.
3. Stir in the sour cream, lemon rind, baking soda, lemon flavoring and vanilla.
4. Add just enough flour to form a soft dough.
5. Drop by the spoonful onto a buttered cookie sheet.
6. Bake in a 350°F (180°C) oven for about 15 minutes or until they turn into a pale cream color. Makes about 6 dozen.

Grandma's Sugar Cookies

½ cup (125 g) butter
½ cup (125 g) lard
1 cup sugar
2 eggs
2 tablespoons sour cream
1¼ teaspoons vanilla

1½ teaspoons grated lemon rind
1 teaspoon baking soda
1 teaspoon baking powder
⅛ teaspoon salt
all-purpose flour
sugar

1. Cream together the butter, lard and sugar until light and fluffy.
2. Add the eggs one at a time beating well after each addition.
3. Stir in the sour cream, vanilla, lemon rind, baking soda, baking powder and salt.
4. Add just enough flour to make a soft dough — about 1¼ cups. Chill for an hour.
5. Roll out on a floured board to a thickness of ¼ inch (5 mm). Cut into rounds and place on a buttered cookie sheet.
6. Bake in a 325°F (160°C) oven for about ten minutes or until they turn into a pale golden color. Sprinkle with sugar while still hot.

Makes about 3 dozen.

Scandinavian Christmas Cookies

1½ cups (375 g) butter
1½ cups sugar
1 egg
1 egg yolk
2½ cups all-purpose flour

½ teaspoon ground cardamom
½ teaspoon cinnamon
¼ teaspoon nutmeg
1 cup ground almonds
1 tablespoon orange juice

1. Cream together the butter and sugar until light and fluffy.
2. Add the egg and egg yolk and beat well.
3. Sift together the flour, cardamom, cinnamon and nutmeg and add to the creamed mixture.
4. Stir in the almonds and orange juice. Blend thoroughly. Chill for at least an hour.
5. Roll out the dough on a floured board to a thickness of ¼ inch (5 mm). Cut into shapes and place on a buttered cookie sheet.
6. Bake in a 400°F (200°C) oven for about five minutes.

Makes about 4 dozen.

Macadamian Balls

½ cup (125 g) butter
½ cup sugar
1 egg yolk, beaten
1½ teaspoons grated lemon rind
1¼ tablespoons lemon juice
1¼ teaspoons vanilla

1 cup ground macadamian nuts
1¼ cups all-purpose flour
1 egg white
ground almonds
confectioners' sugar

1. Cream together the butter and sugar until light and fluffy.
2. Add the egg yolk and beat well.
3. Stir in the grated lemon rind, lemon juice, vanilla, macadamian nuts and flour. Blend thoroughly.
4. Form into small balls.
5. Beat the egg white until frothy.
6. Mix together some ground almonds and confectioners' sugar.
7. Roll the balls first in the egg white then in the almond and sugar mixture. Place on a buttered cookie sheet.
8. Bake in a 350°F (180°C) oven for about 15 minutes. Makes 3 dozen.

New Orleans Pecan Balls

1 cup (250 g) butter
⅓ cup confectioners' sugar
2 teaspoons vanilla
2 cups finely chopped pecans
2 cups all-purpose flour
confectioners' sugar

1. Cream together the butter and ⅓ cup confectioners' sugar until light and fluffy.
2. Add the vanilla and mix thoroughly.
3. Mix together the nuts and flour and add to the mixture. Blend well.
4. Shape into small balls and place on a buttered cookie sheet.
5. Bake in a 275°F (140°C) oven for about ½ hour or until they turn into a pale cream color. Allow to cool, then roll in confectioners' sugar.

Makes about 5 dozen.

Almond Cakes

½ cup (125 g) butter
2½ tablespoons confectioners'
    sugar
2 cups all-purpose flour
¾ cup ground almonds
1 teaspoon almond extract
confectioners' sugar

1. Cream together the butter and sugar until light and fluffy.
2. Mix together the flour and almonds and add to the creamed mixture.
3. Stir in the almond extract and blend well.
4. Shape into small cakes and place on a buttered cookie sheet.
5. Bake in a 350°F (180°C) oven for about eight minutes. Sprinkle with confectioners' sugar.

Makes about 4 dozen.

Fig Cakes

½ cup (125 ml) melted butter
1 cup brown sugar
1¼ cups all-purpose flour
1¼ cups rolled oats
1 teaspoon baking soda
¼ teaspoon salt

Filling:
1 cup chopped figs
½ cup (125 ml) water
½ cup sugar

1. Mix together the melted butter, sugar, flour, oats, baking soda and salt.
2. Spread half the mixture (it will be crumbly) on the bottom of an 8-inch x 10-inch (20-cm x 25-cm) buttered pan.
3. Mix together the figs, water and sugar in a small saucepan. Bring to the boil. Reduce the heat, cover and simmer for three minutes. Remove from the heat and mash.
4. Spoon the filling over the layer of crumbs and cover with the rest of the mixture.
5. Bake in a 300°F (150°C) oven for about ½ hour. Cool before cutting into squares. Makes about 20.

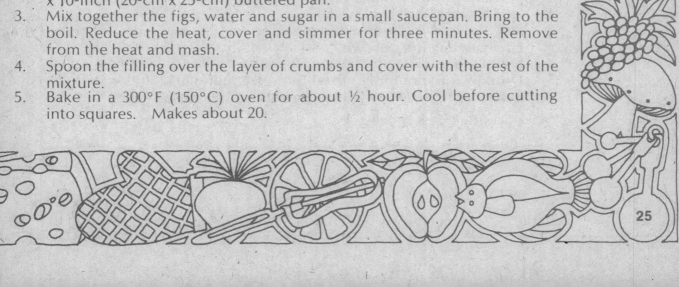

25

Pineapple Cookies

½ cup (125 g) butter
1 cup brown sugar
1 egg, beaten
½ cup crushed pineapple, drained
¾ cup raisins

1¼ teaspoons vanilla
2 cups all-purpose flour
1 teaspoon baking powder
1 teaspoon baking soda
¼ teaspoon salt

1. Cream together the butter and sugar until light and fluffy.
2. Add the egg and beat well.
3. Stir in the pineapple, raisins and vanilla.
4. Sift together the flour, baking powder, baking soda and salt and add to the mixture.
5. Drop by the spoonful onto a buttered cookie sheet.
6. Bake in a 375°F (190°C) oven for about ten minutes.

Makes about 3 dozen.

Fruity Oatmeal Cookies

¾ cup (185 g) butter
1 cup sugar
2 eggs, beaten
2 cups all-purpose flour
¼ teaspoon salt
1 teaspoon cinnamon

¾ teaspoon baking soda
2 cups rolled oats
½ cup raisins
½ cup candied orange and lemon peel

1. Cream the butter and sugar until light and fluffy.
2. Add the eggs and beat well.
3. Sift the flour with the salt, cinnamon and baking soda and add to the creamed mixture. Mix well.
4. Stir in the rolled oats, raisins and peel.
5. Drop by the spoonful onto a buttered cookie sheet.
6. Bake in a 325°F (160°C) oven for about 20 minutes.

Makes about 4 dozen.

Raisin Sandwich Cookies

½ cup (125 g) butter
1 cup sugar
1 egg, beaten
3½ cups all-purpose flour
1 teaspoon baking powder
1 teaspoon baking soda
⅛ teaspoon salt

Filling:
½ cup sugar
½ cup (125 ml) water
1 cup chopped raisins
1 tablespoon all-purpose flour

1. Cream together the butter and sugar until light and fluffy.
2. Add the egg and beat well.
3. Sift together the flour, baking powder, baking soda and salt and add to the creamed mixture. Chill for at least an hour.
4. Make the filling by cooking together all the filling ingredients until soft. Mash and allow to cool.
5. Roll the cookie dough out on a floured board to a thickness of ⅛ inch (3 mm). Place on a buttered cookie sheet.
6. Bake in a 350°F (180°C) oven for about 15 minutes.
7. While still warm spread with the filling and sandwich together.

Makes about 2 dozen.

Walnut Balls

1 cup (250 g) butter
⅔ cup confectioners' sugar
2 teaspoons vanilla
⅔ cup chopped walnuts
2 cups all-purpose flour
confectioners' sugar

1. Cream together the butter and sugar until light and fluffy.
2. Add the vanilla, walnuts and flour. Mix thoroughly.
3. Form into small balls and place on a buttered cookie sheet.
4. Bake in a 275°F (140°C) oven for about ½ hour. Remove from the oven and cool completely before rolling in confectioners' sugar.

Makes about 3 dozen.

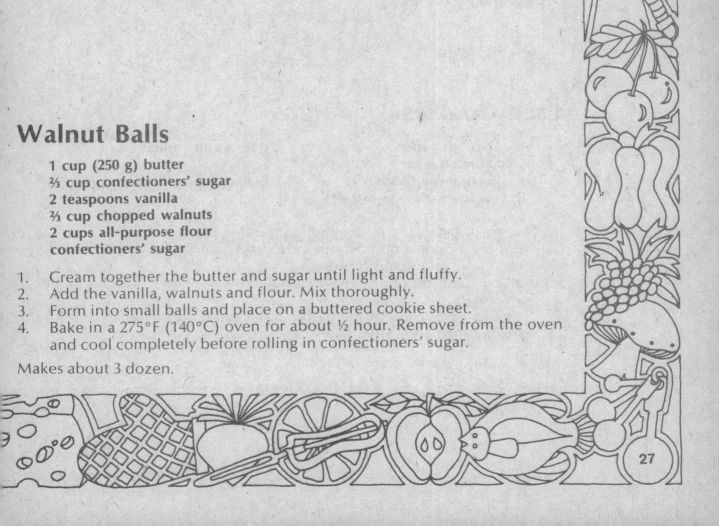

Date-Nut Swirls

1 cup (250 g) butter	**Filling:**
2 cups brown sugar	20 pitted dates, sliced
3 eggs, beaten	½ cup sugar
4½ cups all-purpose flour	½ cup (125 ml) water
1¼ teaspoons cinnamon	1 cup finely crushed nuts
½ teaspoon baking soda	
pinch of salt	

1. Make the filling first by mixing together all the filling ingredients in a saucepan. Bring to the boil, reduce the heat and simmer for five minutes. Allow to cool.
2. Cream together the butter and sugar until light and fluffy.
3. Add the eggs and beat well.
4. Sift together the flour, cinnamon, baking soda and salt. Add to the mixture.
5. Divide the dough into equal halves. Roll out each half on a floured board in a rectangular shape.
6. Spread each half with the filling then roll up tightly. Wrap in wax paper and chill for several hours.
7. Slice thinly and place on a buttered cookie sheet.
8. Bake in a 375°F (190°C) oven for about 15 minutes.

Makes about 3 dozen.

Lace Cookies

¼ cup (65 g) butter	1 teaspoon vanilla
1 cup brown sugar	1 egg, beaten
1 cup ground almonds	4 tablespoons all-purpose flour
1¼ teaspoons almond extract	

1. Cream together the butter and sugar until light and fluffy.
2. Add the ground almonds, almond extract, vanilla and egg. Beat well.
3. Add the flour and mix thoroughly.
4. Drop by the spoonful onto a buttered cookie sheet about 3 inches (8 cm) apart.
5. Bake in a 375°F (190°C) oven for about ten minutes. Remove from the sheet immediately after taking out of the oven.

Makes about 3 dozen.

Butterscotch-Pecan Cookies

½ cup (125 g) butter
½ cup sugar
½ cup brown sugar
2 eggs, beaten

¼ teaspoon salt
½ teaspoon baking powder
½ cup all-purpose flour
1 cup chopped pecans

1. Cream together the butter and sugars until light and fluffy.
2. Add the eggs and beat well.
3. Sift together the salt, baking powder and flour and add to the mixture.
4. Add the pecans and blend thoroughly.
5. Drop by the spoonful onto a buttered cookie sheet.
6. Bake in a 325°F (160°C) oven for about seven minutes.

Makes about 2 dozen.

Pfeffernuesse

1 cup (250 ml) corn syrup
½ cup (125 ml) molasses
¼ cup (65 g) lard
¼ cup (65 g) butter
1¼ teaspoons baking soda
¼ cup (65 ml) hot water

¼ lb (125 g) ground almonds
⅓ cup candied orange and lemon
  peel
1 teaspoon cinnamon
½ teaspoon mixed spice
½ teaspoon nutmeg
4 cups all-purpose flour

1. Mix together the corn syrup, molasses, lard and butter in a large saucepan. Bring to the boil and then remove from the heat. Allow to cool slightly.
2. Mix the baking soda with the hot water.
3. Add to the corn syrup mixture with the ground almonds, peel, cinnamon, mixed spice and nutmeg.
4. Gradually add the flour, mixing constantly.
5. Form into small balls and place on a buttered cookie sheet.
6. Bake in a 325°F (160°C) oven for about 15 minutes or until golden. (Roll in confectioners' sugar, if desired.)

Makes about 3 dozen.

Oatmeal Rounds

2 cups ground oats
1 cup brown sugar
1 cup all-purpose flour
¼ teaspoon salt
½ cup (125 g) butter

½ cup (125 g) lard
1 teaspoon baking soda
¼ cup (65 ml) hot water
1¼ teaspoons vanilla

1. Mix together the oats, sugar, flour and salt.
2. Melt the butter and lard and add to the dry ingredients. Mix well.
3. Dissolve the baking soda in the hot water and add to the mixture with the vanilla.
4. Form into a roll and wrap in wax paper. Chill for at least an hour.
5. Slice thinly and place on a buttered cookie sheet.
6. Bake in a 375°F (190°C) oven for about ten minutes.

Makes about 4 dozen.

Egg White Wafers

½ cup (125 g) butter
½ cup sugar
1 cup all-purpose flour
1¼ teaspoons vanilla

½ cup ground almonds
5 egg whites
⅛ teaspoon salt

1. Cream together the butter and sugar until light and fluffy.
2. Add the flour and mix well.
3. Stir in the vanilla and ground almonds.
4. Beat the egg whites with the salt until stiff but not dry. Fold into the mixture.
5. Drop by the spoonful onto a buttered cookie sheet.
6. Bake in a 325°F (160°C) oven for about 20 minutes or until they turn into a cream color.

Makes about 4 dozen.

Golden Fries

8 egg yolks
3 tablespoons sugar
½ cup (125 ml) cream
½ teaspoon ground cardamom
2 tablespoons brandy
3¼ cups all-purpose flour
oil for deep frying

1. Beat the egg yolks until pale yellow and thick.
2. Add the sugar and cream and beat well.
3. Stir in the cardamom and brandy.
4. Gradually add the flour blending thoroughly. Chill the dough for several hours.
5. Roll out on a floured board to a thickness of about ½ inch (one cm). Cut into diamond shapes.
6. Deep fry in the hot oil until golden brown — about two minutes.

Makes about 4 dozen.

Chocolate Macaroons

½ lb (250 g) grated chocolate
2¼ cups sugar
½ lb (250 g) ground almonds
1½ tablespoons grated lemon
   rind
1¼ teaspoons cinnamon
⅓ cup (85 ml) dry sherry
5 egg whites

1. Mix together the chocolate, sugar, almonds, lemon rind, cinnamon and sherry. Blend thoroughly.
2. Beat the egg whites until stiff and gently fold into the mixture.
3. Drop by the spoonful onto a buttered cookie sheet.
4. Bake in a 350°F (180°C) oven until firm.

Makes about 3 dozen.

Vanilla Nuts

½ cup (125 g) butter
1 cup sugar
4 egg yolks, beaten
3 cups all-purpose flour
¼ lb (125 g) ground almonds
1¼ teaspoons vanilla

1. Cream together the butter and sugar until light and fluffy.
2. Add the egg yolks and beat well.
3. Stir in the flour and almonds.
4. Add the vanilla and blend thoroughly. Chill for several hours.
5. Roll out the dough on a floured board and cut into shapes desired. Place on a buttered cookie sheet.
6. Bake in a 350°F (180°C) oven for about ten minutes or until a golden brown.

Makes about 4 dozen.

Chocolate Date Cookies

⅓ cup (85 g) butter
1¼ cups brown sugar
1 egg, beaten
½ cup (125 ml) milk
½ cup ground chocolate
1¼ teaspoons vanilla

1½ cups all-purpose flour
1 teaspoon baking powder
½ teaspoon baking soda
½ teaspoon cinnamon
1 cup chopped walnuts
1 cup chopped dates

1. Cream together the butter and sugar until light and fluffy.
2. Add the egg, milk, chocolate and vanilla and beat well.
3. Sift together the flour, baking powder, baking soda and cinnamon and add to the mixture. Blend thoroughly.
4. Add the walnuts and dates and mix well.
5. Drop by the spoonful onto a buttered cookie sheet.
6. Bake in a 375°F (190°C) oven for about 12 minutes.

Makes about 3 dozen.

Choc-Almond Cookies

1¼ cups ground browned
    almonds
1 teaspoon almond extract
1 oz (30 g) cooking chocolate
⅔ cup (165 ml) sweetened
    condensed milk

1. Put the almonds in a hot oven to brown them before grinding them.
2. Melt the chocolate with the almond extract in the top of a double boiler over hot water.
3. Add the ground almonds and sweetened condensed milk. Mix well.
4. Drop by the spoonful onto a buttered cookie sheet. Don't put too close together because they will spread.
5. Bake in a 325°F (160°C) oven for about ten minutes.

Makes about 2 dozen.

Orange Cookies

2 cups cake flour
⅛ teaspoon salt
½ cup (125 g) butter
⅔ cup sugar
1 egg
1 teaspoon grated orange rind
½ teaspoon grated lemon rind

1. Sift together the flour and salt. Set aside.
2. Cream together the butter and sugar until light and fluffy.
3. Add the egg, orange and lemon rinds and mix well.
4. Gradually add the flour mixture and blend thoroughly.
5. Form into a roll and wrap in wax paper. Chill for several hours.
6. Cut into thin slices and place on a buttered cookie sheet.
7. Bake in a 400°F (200°C) oven for about ten minutes.

Makes about 3 dozen.

Apricot Cookies

⅓ cup (85 g) butter
1 cup brown sugar
¼ cup (65 ml) milk
1 egg, beaten
1¼ teaspoons vanilla
1 cup chopped dried apricots, soaked

⅓ cup ground nuts
1¾ cups all-purpose flour
⅛ teaspoon salt
½ teaspoon baking powder
½ teaspoon baking soda
1¼ teaspoons cinnamon

1. Cream together the butter and sugar until light and fluffy.
2. Add the milk, egg and vanilla and beat well.
3. Purée the apricots and add to the mixture with the ground nuts.
4. Sift together the flour, salt, baking powder, baking soda and cinnamon and add to the mixture. Blend thoroughly.
5. Drop by the spoonful onto a buttered and floured cookie sheet.
6. Bake in a 350°F (180°C) oven for about ten minutes.

Makes about 3 dozen.

Iced Chocolate Circles

½ cup (125 g) butter
½ cup sugar
1 egg yolk
¾ cup cake flour
1 cup custard powder
2 tablespoons cocoa
milk

Icing:
⅔ cup confectioners' sugar
2 teaspoons cocoa
hot water

1. Cream together the butter and sugar until light and fluffy.
2. Add the egg yolk and beat well.
3. Sift together the flour, custard powder and cocoa and add to the creamed mixture.
4. Add just enough milk to make a firm dough.
5. Roll out on a floured board to a thickness of ¼ inch (5 mm). Cut into rounds then remove the centers with a small round cutter. Place the circles on a buttered cookie sheet.
6. Bake in a 400°F (200°C) oven for about 15 minutes. Remove from the oven and cool completely on a wire rack.
7. Mix the cocoa with just enough hot water to dissolve it, then mix into the confectioners' sugar. Add a little more water if necessary.
8. Spread the icing on the chocolate circles and set aside to harden.

Makes about 2 dozen.

Walnut Cookies

1 cup all-purpose flour
½ teaspoon baking powder
⅛ teaspoon salt
1½ tablespoons (30 g) butter
1½ tablespoons (30 g) lard

½ cup brown sugar
1 egg
1¼ teaspoons vanilla
⅔ cup chopped walnuts

1. Sift together the flour, baking powder and salt. Set aside.
2. Cream together the butter, lard and brown sugar until light and fluffy.
3. Beat in the egg and vanilla.
4. Add the sifted dry ingredients and blend thoroughly.
5. Stir in the chopped walnuts and mix well.
6. Form in long rolls and wrap in wax paper. Chill for several hours.
7. Slice thinly and place on a buttered cookie sheet.
8. Bake in a 400°F (200°C) oven for about ten minutes.

Makes about 3 dozen.

Apricot-Nut Delights

½ cup (125 g) butter
1¼ cups all-purpose flour
¼ cup sugar
water

Filling:
½ cup (125 g) butter
1¼ cups confectioners' sugar
¼ teaspoon vanilla
1½ tablespoons milk
sieved apricot jam
crushed walnuts

1. Rub the butter into the flour and sugar.
2. Add just enough water to form a stiff dough.
3. Roll out on a floured board to a thickness of ¼ inch (5 mm). Cut into rounds and place on a buttered cookie sheet.
4. Bake in a 325°F (160°C) oven for about 20 minutes. Remove from the oven and cool completely on a wire rack.
5. Blend together the butter, sugar and vanilla until smooth.
6. Add the milk a little at a time until smooth and creamy.
7. Spread the filling on half the cookies and sandwich together.
8. Coat the top and the sides of the sandwiches with the sieved apricot jam.
9 Roll the cookies in crushed walnuts to coat the sides.

Makes about one dozen.

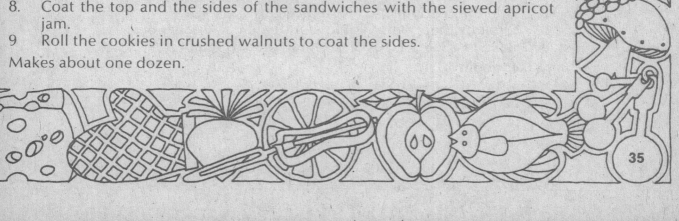

Mocha Cookies

1 cup cake flour
3 tablespoons cocoa
⅛ teaspoon salt
½ cup (125 g) butter
⅓ cup sugar
2 teaspoons instant coffee powder
1 tablespoon hot water

Filling:
4 tablespoons cocoa
3 tablespoons confectioners' sugar
¼ cup (65 ml) black coffee
¼ cup (65 g) butter
confectioners' sugar

1. Sift the flour with the cocoa and salt. Set aside.
2. Cream together the butter and sugar until light and fluffy.
3. Blend the instant coffee powder with the hot water and stir into the butter and sugar mixture.
4. Add the sifted dry ingredients and mix well.
5. Form into small balls and place on a buttered cookie sheet about 2 inches (5 cm) apart. Gently press down with a fork.
6. Cook in a 350°F (180°C) oven for about 15 minutes. Allow to cool for a few minutes before removing from the sheet to a wire rack to cool completely.
7. Mix together the cocoa, confectioners' sugar and black coffee in a small saucepan. Heat gently and mix until thick and creamy. Remove from the heat and cool slightly.
8. Add the butter and mix well.
9. Spread the filling between two cookies and sprinkle with confectioners' sugar.

Makes about one dozen.

Coconut Chews

½ cup (125 ml) condensed milk
¼ teaspoon vanilla
⅛ teaspoon salt
2½ cups shredded coconut

1. Blend together the condensed milk, vanilla and salt.
2. Add the coconut and mix thoroughly.
3. Drop by the spoonful onto a buttered cookie sheet.
4. Bake in a 350°F (180°C) oven for about ten minutes.

Makes about 18.

Lemon Fingers

½ cup (125 g) butter
½ cup sugar
1 egg
1½ tablespoons grated lemon
    rind
2 cups all-purpose flour

Lemon Icing:
½ cup (125 g) butter
1¼ cups confectioners' sugar
1½ teaspoons grated lemon rind
lemon juice
sugar

1. Cream together the butter and sugar until light and fluffy.
2. Add the egg and lemon rind and beat well.
3. Sift the flour and add to the mixture. Blend thoroughly.
4. Pipe the mixture in finger lengths onto a buttered cookie sheet.
5. Bake in a 375°F (190°C) oven for about 20 minutes. Cool completely.
6. Make the Lemon Icing by thoroughly mixing together the butter, sugar, grated lemon rind and just enough lemon juice to make a spreading consistency.
7. When the cookies are cool, sandwich together with the Lemon Icing. Sprinkle generously with sugar.

Makes about one dozen.

Melting Moments

1 cup (250 g) butter
¾ cup sugar
1 egg
½ teaspoon vanilla
2 cups cake flour
cornflake crumbs

1. Cream together the butter and sugar until light and fluffy.
2. Add the egg and vanilla and beat well.
3. Sift the flour and add to the mixture. Blend thoroughly.
4. Shape into small balls and roll in the cornflake crumbs.
5. Place on a buttered cookie sheet and bake in a 375°F (190°C) oven for about 15 minutes.

Makes about 4 dozen.

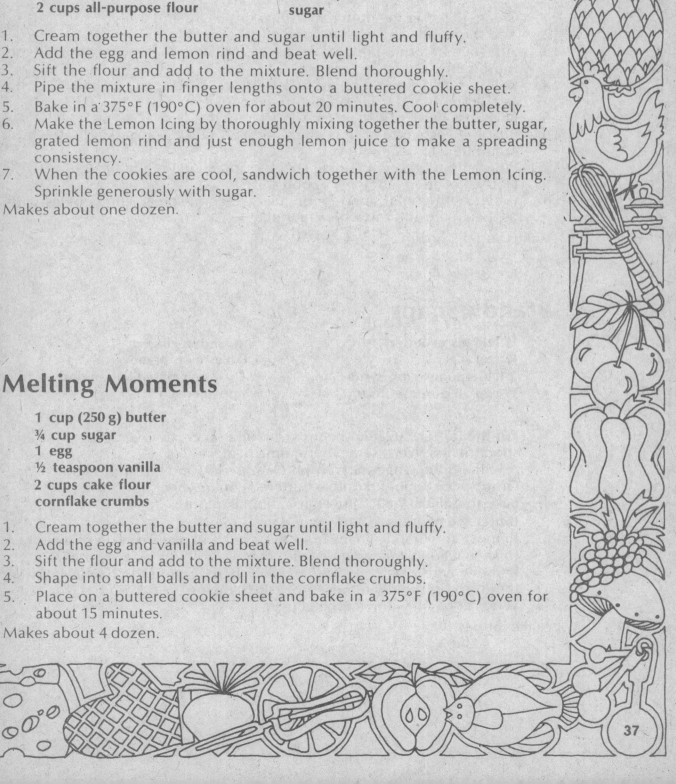

Meringue Toppers

¼ cup (65 g) butter	2 tablespoons cocoa
¼ cup sugar	¼ cup sugar
¼ teaspoon vanilla	⅛ teaspoon salt
1 egg, separated	raspberry jam
¾ cup all-purpose flour	

1. Cream together the butter and sugar until light and fluffy.
2. Add the vanilla and egg yolk and mix thoroughly.
3. Sift together the flour and cocoa and add to the mixture. Blend thoroughly.
4. Roll out on a floured board to a thickness of ⅛ inch (3 mm). Cut into small rounds and place on a buttered cookie sheet.
5. Bake in a 400°F (200°C) oven for five minutes.
6. Beat the egg white until frothy. Gradually add the sugar and salt whilst continuing to beat until stiff.
7. Pipe onto a buttered cookie sheet in small circles and bake in a 300°F (150°C) oven for about 45 minutes.
8. When both cookies and meringues are cool, spread the cookies with raspberry jam and top with a meringue.

Makes about 2 dozen.

Brandy Snaps

¼ cup (65 g) butter	¼ teaspoon ginger
¼ cup sugar	1 tablespoon brandy
2 tablespoons corn syrup	½ teaspoon grated lemon rind
½ cup all-purpose flour	whipped cream

1. Put the butter, sugar and corn syrup in a saucepan over a low heat and stir until dissolved. Remove from the heat.
2. Add the flour, ginger, brandy and lemon rind and mix thoroughly.
3. Drop by the spoonful onto a buttered cookie sheet.
4. Bake in a 350°F (180°C) oven for about 8 minutes.
5. Butter the handles of a few wooden spoons.
6. Remove the Brandy Snaps from the oven and place on top of the stove to keep warm while working with them.
7. Remove with a palette knife and roll them around the handles. When they are cool, gently remove from the handles.
8. When cool, fill with whipped cream.

Makes about 18.

Choc-Logs

1 cup all-purpose flour
⅛ teaspoon salt
½ cup (125 g) butter
1½ tablespoons sugar
3 tablespoons cocoa
½ teaspoon vanilla
cream

Chocolate Icing:
¼ cup (65 g) butter
¾ cup confectioners' sugar
¼ teaspoon vanilla
1 tablespoon cocoa
milk
confectioners' sugar

1. Sift together the flour and salt.
2. Rub in the butter.
3. Add the sugar, cocoa and vanilla.
4. Stir in just enough cream to bind the dough.
5. Put the dough on a lightly floured board and shape into a long roll about one inch (2½ cm) in diameter. Cut into logs 2 inches (5 cm) in length.
6. Place on a buttered cookie sheet and bake in a 375°F (190°C) oven for about ½ hour. Remove from the cookie sheet and cool.
7. To make the icing, mix together the butter and sugar thoroughly. Add the vanilla and cocoa and just enough milk to make it a spreading consistency.
8. When the logs are cool, spread with the Chocolate Icing. Score with the prongs of a fork and sprinkle with confectioners' sugar.

Makes about a dozen.

Gingernuts

1⅓ cups all-purpose flour
⅛ teaspoon salt
1 teaspoon ginger
1 teaspoon mixed spice
1 teaspoon cinnamon

¼ cup (65 g) butter
⅔ cup brown sugar
1 tablespoon molasses
1½ teaspoons grated fresh ginger

1. Sift together the flour, salt, ginger, mixed spice and cinnamon. Set aside.
2. Cream together the butter and sugar until light and fluffy.
3. Add the molasses and fresh ginger. Mix well.
4. Stir in the sifted dry ingredients. The mixture should be stiff but if it is too stiff, add a little more molasses.
5. Roll into small balls and place on a buttered cookie sheet. Press gently to flatten slightly.
6. Bake in a 375°F (190°C) oven for about 20 minutes.

Makes about 2 dozen.

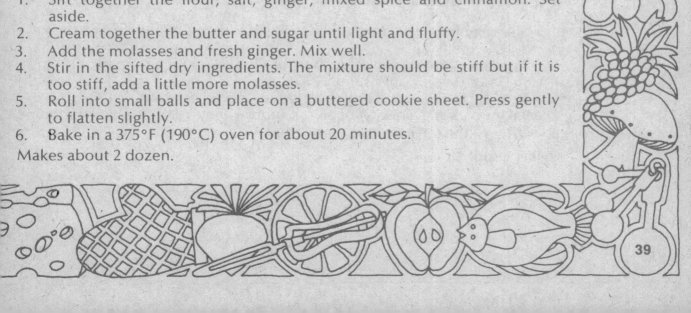

Marshmallow Creams

1½ cups all-purpose flour	milk
⅛ teaspoon salt	1¼ tablespoons corn syrup
½ cup (125 g) butter	½ teaspoon vanilla
½ cup sugar	raspberry jam
1 egg, separated	chopped nuts

1. Sift together the flour and salt and set aside.
2. Cream together the butter and sugar until light and fluffy.
3. Add the egg yolk and beat well.
4. Stir in the sifted dry ingredients.
5. Add just enough milk to form a soft dough.
6. Roll out on a floured board and cut into 1½-inch (4-cm) rounds.
7. Place on a buttered cookie sheet, prick with a fork and bake in a 350°F (180°C) oven for about 15 minutes.
8. Beat the egg white with the corn syrup in the top of a double boiler over hot water until stiff. Add the vanilla and mix well.
9. When the cookies are cool, sandwich together with the raspberry jam.
10. Spread the tops with the meringue and sprinkle with the chopped nuts.

Makes about a dozen.

Nut Rocks

⅔ cup confectioners' sugar
2 egg whites
½ teaspoon vanilla
⅔ cup finely chopped walnuts

1. Mix together the confectioners' sugar and egg whites in the top of a double boiler.
2. Place over boiling water and beat until stiff. Remove from heat.
3. Stir in the vanilla and walnuts.
4. Drop by the spoonful onto a buttered floured cookie sheet.
5. Bake in a 300°F (150°C) oven for about ½ hour. The cookies should be crisp on the outside and soft on the inside.

Makes about 18 cookies.

Cinnamon Curls

½ cup (125 g) butter
½ cup sugar
2 egg whites

1 teaspoon cinnamon
¼ teaspoon nutmeg
1 cup all-purpose flour

1. Cream together the butter and sugar until light and fluffy.
2. Add the egg whites a little at a time beating constantly.
3. Beat in the cinnamon and nutmeg.
4. Sift the flour and add to the mixture. Blend thoroughly.
5. Using a ¼ (5-mm) tube, pipe the mixture onto a buttered cookie sheet in strips about 7 inches (18 cm) long. Make sure the strips are reasonably far apart because the mixture will spread.
6. Bake in a 400°F (200°C) oven for about 8 minutes. Remove from the oven and immediately twist into curls (wrapping around a pencil, if desired).

Makes about 3 dozen.

Cinnamon Squares

1 cup (250 g) lard
1 cup sugar
1 egg
2 cups all-purpose flour

⅛ teaspoon salt
1 tablespoon cinnamon
½ teaspoon nutmeg
chopped nuts

1. Cream together the lard and sugar until light and fluffy.
2. Add the egg and beat well.
3. Sift together the flour, salt, cinnamon and nutmeg and add to the mixture. Blend thoroughly.
4. Press the dough into an 8-inch (20-cm) square buttered pan.
5. Sprinkle on chopped nuts and gently press into the dough.
6. Cook in a 325°F (160°C) oven for about an hour. Cut into squares and allow to cool slightly in the pan before removing to a wire rack to cool completely.

Makes about 16.

Iced Ginger Cookies

½ cup (125 g) butter
⅓ cup molasses
½ cup sugar
2 cups all-purpose flour
3 teaspoons ginger

1 teaspoon baking soda

Icing:
⅔ cup confectioners' sugar
1½ tablespoons warm water

1. Put the butter, molasses and sugar in a saucepan and warm gently. Remove from the heat and beat to a cream.
2. Add the flour, ginger and baking soda and mix to a stiff dough.
3. Roll out on a floured board to a thickness of ¼ inch (5 mm). Cut into rounds and place on a buttered cookie tray.
4. Bake in a 350°F (180°C) oven for about 15 minutes.
5. Make the icing by mixing together the confectioners' sugar and the water.
6. When the cookies are cool, spread on the icing. Decorate with nuts or pieces of preserved ginger.

Makes about 3 dozen.

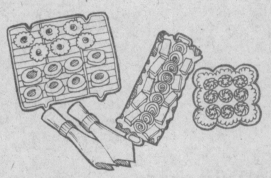

Clover Leaf Cookies

½ cup (125 g) butter
½ cup sugar
1 egg
2 cups all-purpose flour

1 tablespoon caraway seeds
1 teaspoon ginger
1 teaspoon grated lemon rind

1. Cream together the butter and sugar until light and fluffy.
2. Add the egg and beat well.
3. Sift the flour and add to the mixture. Blend thoroughly.
4. Divide the dough into three portions. Add the caraway seeds, to one, the ginger to the next and the lemon rind to the last one.
5. Shape into small balls. Put a ball of each flavour together and place on a buttered cookie sheet. Press down gently to form a clover leaf.
6. Bake in a 400°F (200°C) oven for about ten minutes.

Makes about 3 dozen.

Chocolate Cream Sandwiches

1½ cups all-purpose flour
⅛ teaspoon salt
½ cup sugar
½ cup (125 g) butter
1 egg
½ teaspoon vanilla
milk

Chocolate Cream:
½ cup (125 g) butter
1 cup confectioners' sugar
½ teaspoon vanilla
1½ tablespoons cream
1 tablespoon cocoa
1 tablespoon hot water

1. Sift together the flour and salt. Set aside.
2. Cream together the sugar and butter until light and fluffy.
3. Add the egg and vanilla and beat well.
4. Stir in the sifted dry ingredients.
5. Add just enough milk to form a firm dough.
6. Roll out the dough on a floured board and cut into shapes desired. Place on a buttered cookie sheet.
7. Cook in a 350°F (180°C) oven for about ten minutes.
8. Make the Chocolate Cream by creaming together the butter and sugar until light and fluffy.
9. Stir in the vanilla and cream until smooth.
10. Blend the cocoa with the hot water and add to the mixture.
11. When the cookies are cool, spread the icing on half of them and top with the other half.

Makes about one dozen sandwiches.

Chocolate Walnuts

1½ cups all-purpose flour
2½ tablespoons cocoa
⅛ teaspoon salt
½ cup (125 g) butter
½ cup sugar

1 egg
1 teaspoon vanilla
milk
walnuts, halved

1. Sift together the flour, cocoa and salt. Set aside.
2. Cream together the butter and sugar until light and fluffy.
3. Add the egg and vanilla and beat well.
4. Stir in the sifted dry ingredients and mix thoroughly.
5. Add just enough milk to make a firm dough.
6. Shape into small balls and place on a buttered cookie sheet.
7. Gently press a walnut half into each cookie.
8. Bake in a 350°F (180°C) oven for about 15 minutes.

Makes about 3 dozen.

Prune Cookies

1 cup (250 g) butter
1 cup brown sugar
½ cup sugar
2 eggs
3 teaspoons vinegar
1¼ teaspoons vanilla

1 cup chopped cooked prunes
4 cups all-purpose flour
1 teaspoon baking soda
¾ teaspoon salt
1 cup chopped nuts

1. Cream together the butter and sugars until light and fluffy.
2. Add the eggs one at a time beating well after each addition.
3. Add the vinegar, vanilla and prunes. Blend well.
4. Sift together the flour, baking soda and salt and add to the prune mixture.
5. Add the nuts and mix well.
6. Shape into rolls 2 inches (5 cm) in diameter. Wrap in wax paper and chill for several hours.
7. Cut into thin slices and place on a buttered cookie sheet.
8. Bake in a 400°F (200°C) oven for about ten minutes.

Makes about 9 dozen.

Date Roll-Ups

1 cup (250 g) butter
½ lb (250 g) cream cheese
2 cups all-purpose flour
¼ teaspoon salt
confectioners' sugar
pitted dates

1. Cream together the butter and cream cheese.
2. Sift together the flour and salt and add to the butter and cream cheese mixture. Mix thoroughly. Chill for several hours.
3. Sprinkle a board generously with confectioners' sugar and roll out the dough to a thickness of ⅛ inch (3 mm). Cut into strips 3 inches x 1 inch (8 cm x 2½ cm).
4. Put a date in the center of each strip and roll up. Press the edges together and place on a buttered cookies sheet seam side down.
5. Bake in a 375°F (190°C) oven for about 15 minutes.

Makes about 6 dozen.

Black Eye Susans

½ cup (125 g) butter
½ cup sugar
½ cup brown sugar
1 egg
1 teaspoon vanilla

1 cup smooth peanut butter
1½ cups all-purpose flour
½ teaspoon baking soda
½ teaspoon salt
choc-bits

1. Cream together the butter and sugars until light and fluffy.
2. Add the egg and vanilla and beat well.
3. Stir in the peanut butter.
4. Sift together the flour, baking soda and salt and add to the peanut butter mixture.
5. Force through a cookie press onto a buttered cookie sheet. Press a choc-bit into the center of each cookie.
6. Bake in a 350°F (180°C) oven for about 15 minutes.

Makes about 5 dozen.

Butterscotch Cookies

1 cup (250 g) butter
½ cup sugar
½ cup brown sugar
1 teaspoon vanilla
2 eggs

2¾ cups all-purpose flour
½ teaspoon salt
½ teaspoon baking soda
½ cup finely chopped walnuts

1. Cream together the butter and sugars until light and fluffy.
2. Add the vanilla and eggs one at a time beating well after each addition.
3. Sift together the flour, salt and baking soda and add to the mixture.
4. Stir in the walnuts and mix thoroughly.
5. Form into blocks about 2 inches (5 cm) square. Chill for several hours.
6. Slice about ⅛ inch (3 mm) thick and place on a buttered cookie sheet.
7. Bake in a 400°F (200°C) oven for about seven minutes.

Makes about 5 dozen.

Glazed Almond Cookies

1 cup (250 g) butter
1 cup sugar
½ teaspoon almond extract
½ teaspoon vanilla
2 eggs, separated

¾ cup chopped blanched
   almonds
2⅔ cups cake flour
½ teaspoon salt
whole unblanched almonds

1. Cream together the butter and sugar until light and fluffy.
2. Add the almond extract, vanilla and egg yolks one at a time beating well after each addition.
3. Stir in the chopped nuts.
4. Sift together the flour and salt and add to the mixture. Mix thoroughly. Chill for about an hour.
5. Form into small balls and dip in the unbeaten egg whites. Place on a buttered cookie sheet.
6. Gently press an almond into each cookie.
7. Bake in a 350°F (180°C) oven for about ten minutes.

Makes about 4 dozen.

Peanut Butter Logs

½ cup (125 g) butter
½ cup smooth peanut butter
2 teaspoons grated orange rind
½ cup brown sugar
½ cup sugar
1 egg

½ cup chopped raisins
1 cup all-purpose flour
¼ teaspoon baking soda
½ teaspoon baking powder
½ teaspoon salt
¼ teaspoon cinnamon

1. Cream together the butter and peanut butter.
2. Add the grated orange rind and sugars and beat until light.
3. Add the egg and beat well.
4. Stir in the chopped raisins.
5. Sift together the flour, baking soda, baking powder, salt and cinnamon. Add to the mixture and mix thoroughly. Chill for at least an hour.
6. Form into rolls about 2 inches (5 cm) long and ½ inch (one cm) in diameter. Score the top with the prongs of a fork. Place on a buttered cookie sheet.
7. Bake in a 350°F (180°C) oven for about ten minutes.

Makes 5 dozen.

Rum Balls

1 cup finely crushed vanilla wafers	1½ tablespoons cocoa
1 cup confectioners' sugar	2 tablespoons corn syrup
1½ cups chopped walnuts	¼ cup (65 ml) rum
	½ cup sugar

1. Mix together the wafer crumbs, confectioners' sugar and one cup of the walnuts.
2. Add the cocoa, corn syrup and rum and mix thoroughly.
3. Shape into small balls. Roll half the balls in the remaining nuts and the other half in the sugar. Chill until ready to serve.

Makes about 3 dozen.

Gold Nuggets

½ cup (125 g) butter	½ teaspoon vanilla
⅓ cup sugar	2 teaspoons grated orange rind
1 egg	2 teaspoons grated lemon rind
1¼ cups all-purpose flour	1½ tablespoons orange juice
¼ teaspoon salt	2 teaspoons lemon juice
¼ teaspoon cinnamon	1½ cups chopped walnuts

1. Cream together the butter and sugar until light and fluffy.
2. Add the egg and beat well.
3. Sift together the flour, salt and cinnamon and add to the creamed mixture.
4. Stir in the vanilla, orange and lemon rinds, orange and lemon juices. Mix thoroughly. Chill for at least an hour.
5. Form into small balls and roll in the nuts.
6. Place on a buttered cookie sheet and bake in a 325°F (160°C) oven for about 20 minutes.

Makes about 2 dozen.

Pecan Dainties

1 cup (250 g) butter
½ cup sugar
2 cups all-purpose flour
1¼ teaspoons vanilla

1 tablespoon water
2 cups ground pecans
pecan halves

1. Cream together the butter and sugar until light and fluffy.
2. Sift the flour and add to the creamed mixture.
3. Add the vanilla, water ,and ground pecans. Mix thoroughly. Chill for several hours.
4. Form into small balls and place on a buttered cookie sheet. Lightly press a pecan half into each cookie.
5. Bake in a 325°F (160°C) oven for about 20 minutes.

Makes about 6 dozen.

Oatmeal Cookies

1½ cups brown sugar
¾ cup (185 ml) melted lard
⅓ cup (85 ml) buttermilk
½ teaspoon salt

¾ teaspoon vanilla
1½ cups all-purpose flour
¾ teaspoon baking soda
3 cups quick-cooking oats

1. Beat together the sugar and melted lard.
2. Add the buttermilk, salt and vanilla.
3. Sift together the flour and baking soda and add to the mixture.
4. Stir in the oats blending thoroughly.
5. Shape into small balls and place on a buttered cookie sheet. Gently press down with a fork.
6. Bake in a 375°F (190°C) oven for about ten minutes.

Makes about 5 dozen.

Brazil Nut Cookies

⅔ cup (165 g) butter
1 cup sugar
1 egg
½ teaspoon vanilla
1 teaspoon grated orange rind
1 teaspoon grated lemon rind

1½ tablespoons orange juice
⅔ cup ground Brazil nuts
2 cups all-purpose flour
½ teaspoon baking powder
½ teaspoon salt

1. Cream together the butter and sugar until light and fluffy.
2. Add the egg and vanilla and beat well.
3. Stir in the orange and lemon rinds orange juice and ground Brazil nuts.
4. Sift together the flour, baking powder and salt and add to the mixture. Mix thoroughly.
5. Force through a cookie press onto a buttered cookie sheet.
6. Bake in a 400°F (200°C) oven for about ten minutes.

Makes about 5 dozen.

Cheesy Lemon Cookies

1 cup (250 g) butter
¼ lb (125 g) cream cheese
1 cup sugar
1 egg yolk
1 teaspoon lemon juice

½ teaspoon lemon flavoring
1½ teaspoons grated lemon rind
2½ cups all-purpose flour
½ teaspoon salt

1. Cream together the butter, cream cheese and sugar until light.
2. Add the egg yolk and beat well.
3. Add the lemon juice, lemon flavoring and lemon rind. Mix thoroughly.
4. Sift together the flour and salt and add to the lemon mixture.
5. Force through a cookie press onto a buttered cookie sheet and bake in a 350°F (180°C) oven for about 15 minutes.

Makes about 5 dozen.

49

Spicy Drop Cookies

½ cup (125 g) butter
½ cup brown sugar
2 eggs
½ cup raisins
½ cup chopped dates
1½ cups all-purpose flour
½ teaspoon salt

1½ teaspoons baking powder
2 teaspoons cinnamon
¼ teaspoon cloves
¼ teaspoon nutmeg
1 tablespoon molasses
1½ tablespoons milk

1. Cream together the butter and sugar until light and fluffy.
2. Add the eggs one at a time beating well after each addition.
3. Stir in the raisins and dates.
4. Sift together the flour, salt, baking powder, cinnamon, cloves and nutmeg and add to the mixture alternately with the molasses and milk. Mix thoroughly.
5. Drop by the spoonful onto a buttered cookie sheet.
6. Cook in a 375°F (190°C) oven for about ten minutes.

Makes about 3 dozen.

Sesame Seed Drops

¾ cup (185 g) butter
1½ cups brown sugar
2 eggs
1¼ teaspoons vanilla

1¼ cups all-purpose flour
¼ teaspoon baking powder
pinch salt
½ cup toasted sesame seeds

1. Cream together the butter and sugar until light and fluffy.
2. Add the eggs one at a time beating well after each addition.
3. Stir in the vanilla.
4. Sift together the flour, baking powder and salt and add to the mixture.
5. Add the sesame seeds and mix thoroughly.
6. Bake in a 325°F (160°C) oven for about 15 minutes.

Makes about 3 dozen.

Fudgy Wafers

1 cup (250 g) butter
1 cup sugar
1 egg
2 oz (60 g) cooking chocolate, melted

1¼ teaspoons vanilla
1½ cups all-purpose flour
¼ teaspoon salt
walnut halves

1. Cream together the butter and sugar until light and fluffy.
2. Add the egg and beat well.
3. Stir in the chocolate and vanilla.
4. Sift together the flour and salt and add to the chocolate mixture.
5. Drop by the spoonful onto a buttered cookie sheet. Press a walnut half in the centre of each cookie.
6. Bake in a 400°F (200°C) oven for about ten minutes.

Makes about 5 dozen.

Oat-Peanut Cookies

1 cup (250 g) butter
1 cup sugar
1 cup brown sugar
2 eggs
1¼ teaspoons vanilla

1½ cups all-purpose flour
½ teaspoon baking soda
3 cups quick-cooking oats
½ lb (250 g) salted peanuts

1. Cream together the butter and sugars until light and fluffy.
2. Add the eggs one at a time beating well after each addition.
3. Stir in the vanilla.
4. Sift together the flour and baking soda and mix into the creamed mixture.
5. Stir in the oats and peanuts. Mix thoroughly.
6. Drop by the spoonful onto a buttered cookie sheet.
7. Bake in a 375°F (190°C) oven for about ten minutes.

Makes about 9 dozen.

Mincemeat Hermits

1 cup all-purpose flour
¼ teaspoon baking soda
¼ teaspoon salt
¼ teaspoon nutmeg
¼ teaspoon cinnamon
⅓ cup (85 g) butter
⅓ cup brown sugar
1 egg
½ cup mincemeat
3 teaspoons sour cream

Glaze:
1½ cups confectioners' sugar
pinch salt
1¼ teaspoons vanilla
2 tablespoons (40 ml) melted
   butter
1½ tablespoons cream

1. Sift together the flour, baking soda, salt, nutmeg and cinnamon. Set aside.
2. Cream together the butter and sugar until light and fluffy.
3. Add the egg and beat well.
4. Add the sifted dry ingredients, mincemeat and sour cream. Mix thoroughly.
5. Drop by the spoonful onto a buttered cookie sheet.
6. Bake in a 400°F (200°C) oven for about ten minutes.
7. While the hermits are cooking, make the glaze by mixing together all the glaze ingredients. Stir to a smooth paste. If necessary, add a little more cream.
8. Spread the hermits with the glaze while slightly warm.

Makes about 3 dozen.

Fruity Drops

1 cup (250 g) butter
1 cup brown sugar
2 eggs
1¼ teaspoons vanilla
3 cups all-purpose flour
½ teaspoon baking soda

¼ teaspoon salt
⅓ cup (85 ml) water
1 cup candied orange and lemon
   peel
1 cup chopped dates

1. Cream together the butter and sugar until light and fluffy.
2. Add the eggs one at a time beating well after each addition.
3. Sift together the flour, baking soda and salt. Add to the creamed mixture alternately with the water. Mix well.
4. Add the peel and dates. Mix thoroughly.
5. Drop by the spoonful onto a buttered cookie sheet.
6. Bake in a 400°F (200°C) oven for about ten minutes.

Makes about 4 dozen.

Oatmeal Drops

½ cup (125 g) butter
1 cup sugar
1 egg
1½ cups all-purpose flour
½ teaspoon salt
½ teaspoon baking soda
1 teaspoon cinnamon

½ teaspoon cloves
¼ teaspoon nutmeg
1¾ cups quick-cooking oats
⅔ cup raisins
½ cup chopped nuts
⅓ cup (85 ml) milk

1. Cream together the butter and sugar until light and fluffy.
2. Add the egg and beat well.
3. Sift together the flour, salt, baking soda, cinnamon, cloves and nutmeg.
4. Stir the oats, raisins and nuts into the sifted mixture.
5. Mix together the creamed mixture and oat mixture alternately with the milk. Mix thoroughly.
6. Drop by the spoonful onto a buttered cookie sheet.
7. Bake in a 350°F (180°C) oven for about 15 minutes.

Makes about 3 dozen.

Pine-Nut Drops

4 eggs
1½ cups sugar
½ teaspoon grated lemon rind
½ teaspoon grated orange rind

2¼ cups all-purpose flour
¼ teaspoon salt
⅔ cup pine nuts
confectioners' sugar

1. Put the eggs and sugar in the top of a double boiler over hot water. Beat until the mixture is warm. Remove from heat and continue beating until frothy and cool.
2. Add the grated lemon and orange rinds, flour, salt and pine nuts. Mix thoroughly.
3. Drop by the spoonful onto a buttered cookie sheet. Sprinkle with confectioners' sugar and set aside for ten minutes.
4. Bake in a 375°F (190°C) oven for about ten minutes.

Makes about 4 dozen.

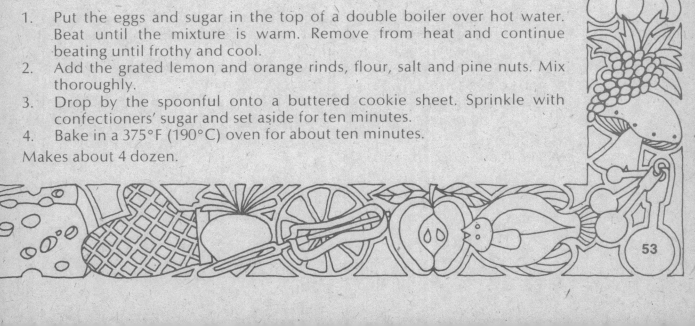

Cherry-Coconut Drops

1 egg white
⅛ teaspoon salt
½ cup sugar

1¼ cups flaked coconut
½ teaspoon vanilla
glacé cherries

1. Beat the egg white until frothy.
2. Add the salt and two tablespoons of sugar at a time. Beat until stiff.
3. Fold in the coconut and vanilla.
4. Drop by the spoonful onto a buttered cookie sheet.
5. Place a glacé cherry in the center of each cookie.
6. Bake in a 350°F (180°C) oven for about 12 minutes.

Makes about a dozen.

Coconut Kisses

½ teaspoon salt
4 egg whites
1¼ cups sugar
1¼ teaspoons vanilla
2 cups shredded coconut

1. Beat together the salt and egg whites until stiff but not dry.
2. Add the sugar one tablespoon at a time while continuing to beat.
3. Fold in the vanilla and coconut.
4. Drop by the spoonful onto brown paper on a cookie sheet.
5. Bake in a 350°F (180°C) oven for about 20 minutes.
6. Wet a cutting board and slide the brown paper with the cookies on it onto the board. Let stand for one minute then remove them from the paper.

Makes about 4 dozen.

Hermits

½ cup (125 g) butter
1 cup brown sugar
2 eggs
2 cups cake flour
1 teaspoon baking powder
½ teaspoon salt

1 teaspoon cinnamon
¼ teaspoon cloves
¼ teaspoon nutmeg
2 cups raisins
½ cup chopped nuts

1. Cream together the butter and sugar until light and fluffy.
2. Add the eggs one at a time beating well after each addition.
3. Sift together the flour, baking powder, salt, cinnamon, cloves and nutmeg. Add to the mixture and blend thoroughly.
4. Stir in the raisins and nuts.
5. Drop by the spoonful onto a buttered cookie sheet.
6. Bake in a 350°F (180°C) oven for about ten minutes.

Makes about 4 dozen.

Butter Wafers

½ cup (125 g) butter
1 cup brown sugar
1¼ teaspoons vanilla
1 egg

¾ cup all-purpose flour
1 teaspoon baking powder
½ teaspoon salt
½ cup chopped nuts

1. Cream together the butter and sugar until light and fluffy.
2. Add the vanilla and egg and beat well.
3. Sift together the flour, baking powder and salt and add to the creamed mixture.
4. Stir in the nuts.
5. Drop by the spoonful onto a buttered cookie sheet.
6. Bake in a 400°F (200°C) oven for about five minutes. Cool slightly before removing from sheet.

Makes about 4 dozen.

Oatmeal Sandwiches

1 cup (250 g) butter
1 cup sugar
1¼ teaspoons vanilla
2 cups finely ground rolled oats
2 cups all-purpose flour
¼ teaspoon baking soda
¾ teaspoon salt
½ cup (125 ml) milk

Filling:
1 lb (500 g) dates, chopped
1½ cups sugar
½ teaspoon salt
3 teaspoons grated lemon rind
2 cups (500 ml) water
2 cups minced nuts

1. Cream together the butter, sugar and vanilla until light and fluffy.
2. Add the oats and mix well.
3. Sift together the flour, baking soda and salt and add to the oat mixture. Blend thoroughly.
4. Add the milk and mix well. Chill for several hours.
5. Roll out on a floured board to a thickness of ⅛ inch (3 mm). Cut into 2-inch (5-cm) rounds and place on a buttered cookie sheet.
6. Bake in a 400°F (200°C) oven for about ten minutes. Remove from the oven and cool.
7. Mix together all the filling ingredients, except the nuts, in a saucepan. Bring to the boil. Reduce the heat and simmer for about ten minutes or until thick. Stir frequently.
8. Mix in the minced nuts and allow to cool.
9. Spread half the cookies with the filling. Top with the other half.

Makes about 6 dozen.

Sweet Sherry Cookies

1 cup (250 g) butter
2 cups sugar
2 egg yolks
5 cups all-purpose flour, sifted

⅛ teaspoon salt
⅔ cup (165 ml) sweet sherry
1 egg white
chopped nuts

1. Mix together the butter, sugar and egg yolks. Beat until light and fluffy.
2. Add the flour and salt alternately with the sherry. Mix well. Chill in the refrigerator for at least ½ hour.
3. Roll out on a floured board and cut into 2-inch (5-cm) rounds. Brush with the slightly beaten egg white and sprinkle with chopped nuts.
4. Bake in a 325°F (160°C) oven for about ten minutes.

Makes about 7 dozen.

Almond Stars

½ cup (125 g) butter	½ teaspoon salt
1 cup sugar	1 teaspoon baking powder
2 eggs, separated	1½ cups all-purpose flour
3 teaspoons milk	almonds
½ teaspoon vanilla	½ teaspoon cinnamon
¼ teaspoon cinnamon	1 tablespoon sugar

1. Cream together the butter and sugar until light and fluffy.
2. Add the egg yolks one at a time beating well after each addition.
3. Stir in the milk and vanilla.
4. Sift together the cinnamon, salt, baking powder and flour and add to the mixture. Mix well. Chill for several hours.
5. Roll out the dough to a thickness of ⅛ inch (3 mm). Cut with a star shaped cookie cutter. Place on a buttered cookie sheet.
6. Put an almond on top of each cookie and press slightly. Brush with slightly beaten egg whites.
7. Mix together the cinnamon and sugar and sprinkle on the top.
8. Bake in a 375°F (190°C) oven for about 8 minutes.

Makes about 3 dozen.

Golden Cookies

1 cup (250 g) butter
⅔ cup sugar
1 teaspoon vanilla
2 eggs
1½ cups all-purpose flour
¼ teaspoon salt

1. Cream together the butter and sugar until light and fluffy.
2. Add the vanilla and eggs one at a time and beat well after each addition.
3. Sift together the flour and salt and add to the mixture.
4. Drop by the spoonful onto a buttered cookie sheet.
5. Bake in a 350°F (180°C) oven for about ten minutes.

Makes about 3 dozen.

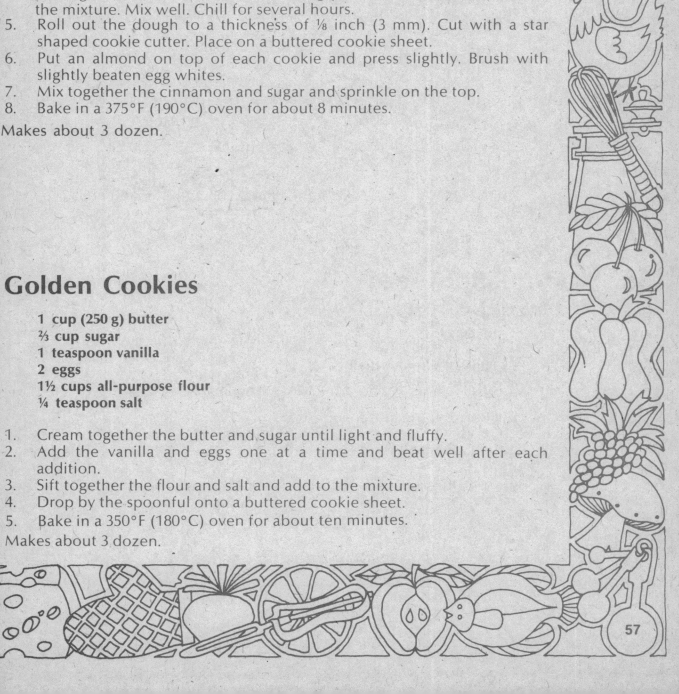

Egg Shortbread

6 cups all-purpose flour
1¼ cups sugar
1 lb (500 g) butter
2 egg yolks

1. Mix together the flour, sugar and butter until thoroughly combined.
2. Add the egg yolks one at a time mixing well after each addition.
3. Divide into 10 parts and roll out each part to a thickness of ½ inch (one cm). Prick with a fork.
4. Bake in a 350°F (180°C) oven for 15 minutes. Reduce the heat to 300°F (150°C) and cook for another ½ hour.
5. Cut into sixths and cook until the edges are golden brown.

Makes 5 dozen.

Nut Shortbread

1 cup (250 g) butter
½ cup sugar
⅛ teaspoon salt
2½ cups all-purpose flour
⅔ cup chopped nuts

1. Mix together the butter and sugar.
2. Sift the salt and flour and add to the creamed mixture.
3. Stir in the chopped nuts and mix until thoroughly blended. Chill for an hour.
4. Roll out to a thickness of ½ inch (one cm). Cut into 1½-inch (4-cm) circles.
5. Bake in a 300°F (150°C) oven for about 20 minutes.

Makes about 2 dozen.

Choc Tops

⅔ cup (165 g) butter
1 cup sugar
1 cup ground walnuts
1 teaspoon vanilla

1½ cups all-purpose flour
½ teaspoon salt
1½ cups choc-bits

1. Cream together the butter and sugar until light and fluffy.
2. Add the walnuts and vanilla and beat well.
3. Sift together the flour and salt and add to the creamed mixture.
4. Because the mixture is very dry, place between two pieces of wax paper and roll out to a thickness of ¼ inch (5 mm).
5. Cut into shapes desired and place on an ungreased cookie sheet.
6. Bake in a 400°F (200°C) oven for about ten minutes. Cool completely.
7. Melt the choc-bits over hot water. Spread on the cookies and cool before serving.

Makes about 4 dozen.

Jam Sandwich Cookies

4 cups all-purpose flour
1 cup (250 g) butter
1¼ cups sugar
¼ teaspoon salt
2 tablespoons cream
4 egg yolks

1½ teaspoons vanilla
1 egg white
½ cup ground nuts
sugar
raspberry jam (or jam of your choice)

1. Sift the flour in a large mixing bowl then mix thoroghly with the butter, sugar, salt, cream, egg yolks and vanilla. Chill for several hours.
2. Roll the dough out on a floured board to a thickness of ⅛ inch (3 mm). Cut into 2-inch (5-cm) circles. Cut holes in the centers of half the circles.
3. Brush the cookies with the holes in them with the slightly beaten egg white. Sprinkle with nuts and sugar.
4. Place all the cookies on buttered cookie sheets and bake in a 350°F (180°C) oven for about ten minutes. Remove from the oven and cool.
5. Spread jam on the plain cookies and top with the ones with holes. Put a little extra jam in the centers.

Makes about 4 dozen.

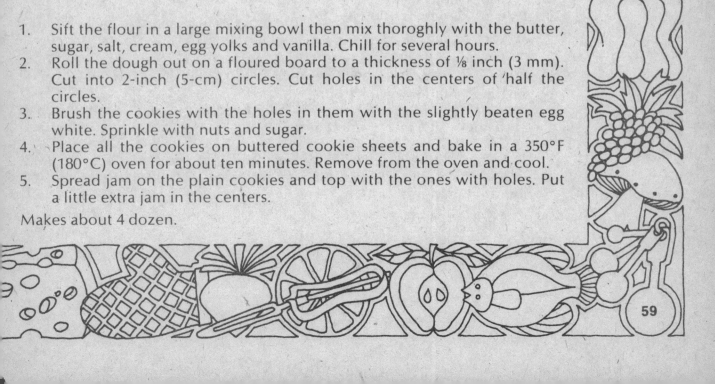

Sugar Rings

1 cup (250 g) butter	1 egg
1 cup sugar	3 cups cake flour
2 teaspoons grated lemon rind	¼ teaspoon salt
2 teaspoons grated orange rind	confectioners' sugar

1. Cream together the butter, sugar and grated rinds until light and fluffy.
2. Add the egg and beat well.
3. Sift together the flour and salt and add to the creamed mixture. Chill for at least an hour.
4. Sprinkle a board generously with confectioners' sugar and roll out the dough to a thickness of ¼ inch (5 mm). Cut into strips about 4 inches x ½ inch (10 cm x 1 cm).
5. Put on an ungreased cookie sheet joining the ends to form rings.
6. Cook in a 400°F (200°C) oven for about ten minutes.

Makes about 4 dozen.

Coconut Rings

½ cup (125 g) butter	1 teaspoon baking powder
½ cup sugar	¼ teaspoon salt
1¼ tablespoons milk	flaked coconut
1⅓ cups all-purpose flour	

1. Cream together the butter and sugar until light and fluffy.
2. Add the milk and beat well.
3. Sift together the flour, baking powder and salt and add to the creamed mixture. Chill for several hours.
4. Sprinkle a board generously with flaked coconut. Roll out the dough to a thickness of ¼ inch (5 mm) and cut into strips 4 inches x ½ inch (10cm x 1 cm).
5. Place on an ungreased cookie sheet and join the ends to form rings. Sprinkle with flaked coconut and bake in a 375°F (190°C) oven for about ten minutes.

Makes about 2 dozen.

Orange-Molasses Cookies

1 cup (250 g) butter
1 cup sugar
1½ tablespoons grated orange
   rind
2 eggs
1 cup molasses

4 cups all-purpose flour
1 teaspoon baking soda
¾ teaspoon salt
1 teaspoon ginger
¼ teaspoon nutmeg
sugar

1. Cream together the butter and sugar until light and fluffy.
2. Add the orange rind and eggs and beat well.
3. Stir in the molasses.
4. Sift together the flour, baking soda, salt, ginger and nutmeg and add to the mixture. Mix thoroughly. Chill for at least one hour.
5. Roll out on a floured board to a thickness of ¼ inch (5 mm).
6. Sprinkle with sugar and roll lightly.
7. Cut into shapes desired and place on a buttered cookie sheet.
8. Bake in a 375°F (190°C) oven for about 10 minutes.

Makes about 2 dozen.

Crispy Ginger Cookies

1 cup (250 g) butter
½ cup sugar
½ cup brown sugar
⅓ cup molasses
⅔ cup light corn syrup
4½ cups all-purpose flour

1 teaspoon baking soda
¾ teaspoon salt
1 teaspoon cinnamon
1½ teaspoons ginger
½ teaspoon cloves

1. Cream together the butter and sugars until light and fluffy.
2. Add the molasses and corn syrup and beat well.
3. Sift together the flour, baking soda, salt, cinnamon, ginger and cloves and mix into the creamed mixture. Mix to a firm dough. Chill for at least one hour.
4. Roll out on a floured board to a thickness of ¼ inch (5 mm).
5. Cut into shapes desired and place on a buttered cookie sheet.
6. Bake in a 350°F (180°C) oven for about eight minutes.

Makes about 5 dozen.

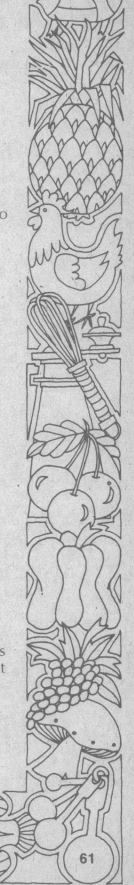

Chocolate Diamonds

2 oz (60 g) cooking chocolate
½ cup (125 g) butter
1 cup sugar
2 eggs

½ cup all-purpose flour
¼ teaspoon salt
¾ teaspoon vanilla
¾ cup chopped walnuts

1. Melt the chocolate and butter in the top of a double boiler over hot water.
2. Add the sugar and mix until the sugar is dissolved. Remove from the heat.
3. Add the eggs one at a time, beating well after each addition.
4. Sift together the flour and salt and add to the mixture with the vanilla.
5. Spread on a 10-inch x 14-inch (25-cm x 35-cm) buttered and floured pan.
6. Sprinkle on the nuts and bake in a 400°F (200°C) oven for about 12 minutes. Cool slightly and cut into diamond shapes.

Makes about 3 dozen.

Seed Cookies

½ cup (125 g) butter
½ cup sugar
2 cups all-purpose flour
1½ teaspoons baking powder

½ teaspoon salt
⅓ cup (85 ml) water
1½ teaspoons poppy seeds
1½ teaspoons caraway seeds

1. Cream together the butter and sugar until light and fluffy.
2. Sift together the flour, baking powder and salt and add to the creamed mixture.
3. Add the water and mix to a smooth dough.
4. Divide the dough in half and roll out each half to a thickness of ¼ inch (5 mm).
5. Sprinkle the poppy seeds on one half and the caraway seeds on the other half. Roll lightly.
6. Cut into shapes desired and place on a buttered cookie sheet.
7. Bake in a 400°F (200°C) oven for about 10 minutes.

Makes about 4 dozen.

Mincemeat Squares

1 tablespoon (20 g) butter
1½ cups brown sugar
2 eggs
2 tablespoons molasses
2 cups all-purpose flour
½ teaspoon baking powder
½ teaspoon baking soda
1 teaspoon cinnamon
¼ teaspoon nutmeg
¼ teaspoon cloves

¼ cup (65 ml) hot water
½ cup chopped nuts
¼ cup chopped raisins
½ lb (250 g) mincemeat

Frosting:
3 cups confectioners' sugar
⅓ cup (85 ml) hot milk
1¼ teaspoons vanilla
pinch salt

1. Mix together the butter, brown sugar, eggs and molasses.
2. Sift together the flour, baking powder, baking soda, cinnamon, nutmeg and cloves and add to the mixture. Blend thoroughly. Add the water and blend.
3. Add half the nuts, the raisins and mincemeat. Mix well.
4. Spread on the bottom of a 9-inch x 14-inch (23-cm x 35-cm) buttered and floured pan.
5. Bake in a 400°F (200°C) oven for 15 minutes.
6. Meanwhile make the frosting by mixing all the ingredients together. Beat until smooth.
7. Remove the mincemeat mixture from the oven and cool slightly.
8. Spread on the frosting while still warm and sprinkle with the rest of the nuts. Cool and cut into squares.

Makes about 3 dozen.

Nutty Date Chews

¾ cup all-purpose flour
¼ teaspoon salt
1 teaspoon baking powder
1 cup sugar

1 cup chopped dates
1 cup chopped walnuts
3 eggs, beaten

1. Sift together the flour, salt, baking powder and sugar.
2. Mix in the dates, walnuts and eggs. Mix thoroughly.
3. Pour into a buttered and floured 10-inch x 14-inch (25-cm x 35-cm) pan.
4. Bake in a 300°F (150°C) oven for about ½ hour. Cool slightly and cut into squares.

Brazil Nut Bars

¼ cup (65 g) butter
1 cup all-purpose flour
½ teaspoon salt
¾ cup brown sugar
2 eggs, beaten
1½ cups finely chopped Brazil nuts

½ cup shredded coconut
1 teaspoon vanilla
6 oz (185 g) cooking chocolate
¼ cup corn syrup
1 tablespoon water

1. Blend together the butter, flour and ¼ teaspoon salt. Press on the bottom of a 9-inch (23-cm) square pan.
2. Bake in a 350°F (180°C) oven for 15 minutes.
3. Beat the sugar with the eggs until thick and creamy.
4. Add the rest of the salt, one cup of the nuts, the coconut and vanilla. Mix thoroughly.
5. Spread over the cooked layers and bake in the oven for another 15 minutes. Remove from the oven and cool in the pan.
6. Melt the chocolate over hot water.
7. Add the corn syrup and water and blend well.
8. Spread on the baked mixture and sprinkle on the rest of the nuts. Allow to stand until firm. Cut into bars.

Makes 2 dozen.

Coconut Squares

½ cup (125 g) butter
1½ cups brown sugar
1¼ cups all-purpose flour
½ teaspoon salt

1 teaspoon vanilla
2 eggs
1 cup chopped nuts
1¼ cups flaked coconut

1. Cream together the butter and ½ cup of sugar until light and fluffy.
2. Add one cup of flour and mix well. Press into a buttered and floured 9-inch x 14-inch (23-cm x 35-cm) pan.
3. Bake in a 375°F (190°C) oven for about 12 minutes.
4. Mix together the rest of the sugar, the rest of the flour, the salt, vanilla, eggs, nuts and coconut.
5. Spread evenly on the mixture in the pan and bake for another 20 minutes. Cut into squares and cool in the pan.

Makes about 3 dozen.

Honey-Date Squares

1 cup (250 g) honey
3 eggs, beaten
1 teaspoon vanilla
1⅓ cups all-purpose flour
1 teaspoon baking powder

¼ teaspoon salt
¾ lb (375 g) pitted dates, chopped
1 cup chopped nuts
sugar

1. Mix together the honey, eggs and vanilla. Beat well.
2. Sift together the flour, baking powder and salt and add to the honey mixture.
3. Stir in the dates and nuts.
4. Spread in a buttered and floured 10-inch (25-cm) square pan.
5. Bake in a 350°F (180°C) oven for about 45 minutes. Cool in the pan then cut into squares and remove from the pan. Roll in sugar.

Makes about 2 dozen.

Spicy Walnut Squares

1 cup (250 g) butter
1 cup brown sugar
1 teaspoon vanilla
1 egg, separated

2 cups all-purpose flour
½ teaspoon salt
1¼ teaspoons cinnamon
1 cup ground walnuts

1. Cream together the butter, sugar and vanilla until light and fluffy.
2. Add the egg yolk and beat well.
3. Sift together the flour, salt and cinnamon and add to the creamed mixture.
4. Stir in half the nuts.
5. Spread the mixture in a buttered and floured 10-inch x 14-inch (25-cm x 35-cm) pan.
6. Beat the egg white until frothy and spoon onto the mixture.
7. Sprinkle with the rest of the nuts.
8. Bake in a 350°F (180°C) oven for about 25 minutes. Cool slightly then cut into squares.

Makes about 2 dozen.

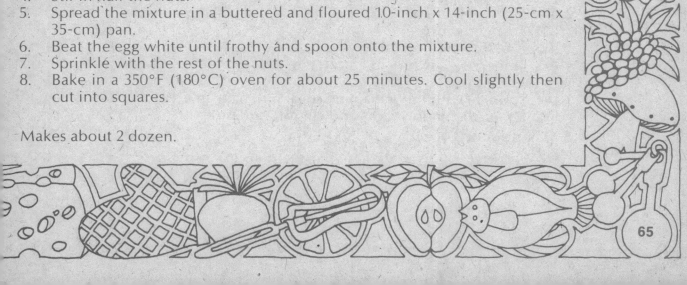

Saucepan Brownies

⅓ cup (85 g) butter
2 oz (60 g) cooking chocolate
½ teaspoon vanilla
1 cup sugar

2 eggs
¾ cup all-purpose flour
¼ teaspoon salt
¾ cup chopped walnuts

1. Put the butter and cooking chocolate into a saucepan and melt over a low heat. Remove from the heat and cool.
2. Add the vanilla and sugar and beat well.
3. Add the eggs one at a time beating well after each addition.
4. Sift together the flour and salt and add to the chocolate mixture.
5. Stir in the walnuts and pour into a buttered and wax paper-lined 8-inch square (20-cm square) pan.
6. Bake in a 350°F (180°C) oven for about 25 minutes. Turn out and remove the paper. Cool and cut into squares.

Makes about 1½ dozen.

Ginger Sugar Squares

1 cup (250 g) butter
1¼ cups sugar
2 eggs
2 cups all-purpose flour

¼ teaspoon baking soda
¼ teaspoon salt
1½ teaspoons ginger
2 tablespoons sour milk

1. Cream together the butter and one cup of the sugar until light and fluffy.
2. Add the eggs one at a time beating well after each addition.
3. Sift together the flour, baking soda, salt and ginger and stir into the creamed mixture.
4. Add the milk and mix well.
5. Spread the mixture in a buttered and floured 9-inch x 14-inch (23-cm x 35-cm) pan.
6. Sprinkle with the remaining sugar and bake in a 400°F (200°C) oven for about 20 minutes. Cool and cut into squares.

Makes about 3 dozen.

Marble Brownies

1 cup (250 g) butter
1½ teaspoons vanilla
2 cups sugar
4 eggs
2 cups all-purpose flour
½ teaspoon salt
2 cups chopped nuts
2 oz (60 g) cooking chocolate, melted and cooled

Chocolate Frosting:
1½ cups confectioners' sugar
3 oz (90 g) cooking chocolate, melted
pinch of salt
2 tablespoons hot water
3 egg yolks
½ teaspoon vanilla
¼ cup (65 g) butter

1. Cream together the butter, vanilla and sugar until light and fluffy.
2. Add the eggs one at a time beating well after each addition.
3. Sift together the flour and salt and mix into the creamed mixture.
4. Stir in the nuts.
5. Divide the batter in half. Pour the melted chocolate into one half and mix well.
6. Drop the batters alternately by the spoonfuls into a buttered, floured and wax paper-lined pan 9-inch x 14-inch (23-cm x 35-cm). Run a knife through the batters to make a marble pattern.
7. Bake in a 350°F (180°C) oven for about 45 minutes. After cooling for about ten minutes in the pan, turn out and cool completely on a wire rack.
8. Make the frosting by mixing half the sugar with the chocolate.
9. Add the salt, water and remaining sugar. Beat well.
10. Beat in the egg yolks one at a time.
11. Add the vanilla and butter and beat thoroughly.
12. Spread the frosting on the brownies and cut into squares when ready to serve.

Makes about 2 dozen.

Coconut-Nut Bars

½ cup (125 g) butter	2 tablespoons all-purpose flour
2 tablespoons confectioners' sugar	¼ teaspoon salt
1 cup cake flour	1½ teaspoons baking powder
2 eggs	1 cup coarsely chopped walnuts
1¼ cups brown sugar	1 cup moist, shredded coconut

1. Blend together the butter, confectioners' sugar and cake flour.
2. Line an 8-inch (20-cm) square pan with wax paper.
3. Spread the mixture in the pan.
4. Bake in a 350°F (180°C) oven for ½ hour.
5. Beat together the eggs and brown sugar until thick and creamy.
6. Sift together the flour, salt and baking powder and add to the egg and sugar mixture.
7. Add the nuts and coconut and spread over the cooked mixture.
8. Return to the oven and cook for another ½ hour. Cut into squares and cool in the pan.

Makes about 2 dozen.

Molasses Creams

½ cup (125 g) butter	½ teaspoon salt
½ cup sugar	1½ teaspoons baking powder
1 egg, beaten	¼ teaspoon baking soda
½ cup molasses	1 teaspoon cinnamon
½ cup (125 ml) hot coffee	½ teaspoon ground cloves
1½ cups all-purpose flour	¼ teaspoon nutmeg

1. Cream together the butter and sugar until light and fluffy.
2. Add the egg and molasses and beat well.
3. Pour in the coffee and beat thoroughly.
4. Sift together flour, salt, baking powder, baking soda, cinnamon, ground cloves and nutmeg. Add to the molasses mixture.
5. Line a 9-inch x 14-inch (23-cm x 35-cm) pan with wax paper.
6. Pour in the mixture and bake in a 350°F (180°C) oven for about ½ hour. Cool and cut into squares.

Makes about 2 dozen.

Orange Squares

1 orange	2 cups all-purpose flour
1 cup raisins	½ teaspoon baking powder
½ cup (125 g) butter	¼ teaspoon salt
1 cup sugar	1½cups confectioners' sugar
1 egg	

1. Halve the orange and squeeze out two tablespoons of the juice. Set aside.
2. Cut the rest of the orange coarsely and put into the electric blender with the raisins. Whirl to chop.
3. Cream together the butter and sugar until light and fluffy.
4. Add the egg and beat well.
5. Sift together the flour, baking powder and salt and add to the creamed mixture.
6. Add the orange and raisins mixture and mix thoroughly.
7. Spread into a buttered and floured 9-inch x 14-inch (23-cm x 35-cm) pan.
8. Bake in a 425°F (220°C) oven for about 25 minutes.
9. Mix together the orange juice and confectioners' sugar. Beat until smooth.
10. Spread the icing on the cooked mixture while still warm. Cool and cut into squares.

Makes about 3 dozen.

Crispie-Coconut Squares

¼ cup (65 g) butter	2 eggs, beaten
½ cup brown sugar	1¼ teaspoons vanilla
1 cup all-purpose flour	¼ teaspoon salt
⅛ teaspoon salt	1 cup moist shredded coconut
¼ teaspoon nutmeg	1 cup rice crispies
¼ teaspoon cinnamon	1 cup chopped walnuts
1 cup brown sugar	

1. Cream together the butter and ½ cup brown sugar until light and fluffy.
2. Sift together the flour, salt, nutmeg and cinnamon. Add to the creamed mixture.
3. Press into a 9-inch square (23-cm square) pan lined with wax paper.
4. Bake in a 350°F (180°C) oven for 15 minutes.
5. Beat the one cup of brown sugar with the eggs until fluffy.
6. Stir in the vanilla, salt, coconut, rice crispies and walnuts. Mix well then spread over the cooked mixture. Bake for another ½ hour. Cut into squares while still warm.

Makes about 16.

Almond Coconut Bars

½ cup (125 g) butter	1 cup all-purpose flour
½ cup sugar	¼ teaspoon salt
1 egg	1 teaspoon baking powder
1 teaspoon vanilla	¼ cup ground almonds
⅔ cup moist shredded coconut	⅓ cup slivered almonds

1. Cream together the butter and sugar until light and fluffy.
2. Add the egg and beat well.
3. Add the vanilla and coconut and mix thoroughly.
4. Sift together the flour, salt and baking powder and stir into the coconut mixture.
5. Add the ground and slivered almonds.
6. Spread into a 10-inch square (25-cm square) pan lined with wax paper.
7. Bake in a 350°F (180°C) oven for about 20 minutes. Cut into bars and remove from the pan while still warm.

Makes about 20.

Oatmeal-Date Bars

½ cup (125 g) butter
1 cup brown sugar
1½ cups all-purpose flour
½ teaspoon salt
1 teaspoon baking soda
1¾ cups quick-cooking oats

Filling:
1 lb (500 g) dates
1 cup sugar
1 cup (250 ml) water
½ teaspoon cinnamon

1. Cream together the butter and sugar until light and fluffy.
2. Sift together the flour, salt and baking soda. Add to the creamed mixture.
3. Stir in the oats and mix until crumbly. Set aside.
4. Pit and chop the dates and mix with the sugar, water and cinnamon in a saucepan. Cook until thick. Cool slightly.
5. Spread half the oat mixture on the bottom of an 8-inch x 14-inch (20-cm x 35-cm) pan lined with wax paper. Press down firmly.
6. Spread on the Date Filling and top with the remaining oat mixture. Press down gently.
7. Bake in a 350°F (180°C) oven for about 20 minutes.

Makes about 18.

Sugar Bars

2 tablespoons (40 g) butter
⅔ cup sugar
1 cup cake flour
⅛ teaspoon salt
1 teaspoon baking powder

1 teaspoon cinnamon
½ cup (125 ml) milk
1 egg, beaten
sugar

1. Cream together the butter and sugar until light and fluffy.
2. Sift together the flour, salt, baking powder and cinnamon and mix into the creamed mixture.
3. Combine the milk and egg and beat into the mixture.
4. Spread on an 8-inch x 14-inch (20-cm x 35-cm) pan lined with wax paper.
5. Bake in a 350°F (180°C) oven for 15 minutes. Sprinkle generously with sugar and bake for another ten minutes. Cut into bars and serve warm or cold.

Makes about 18.

Brownies

½ cup (125 g) butter
2 oz (60 g) cooking chocolate
¾ cup all-purpose flour
½ teaspoon baking powder
½ teaspoon salt

2 eggs
1 cup sugar
1 teaspoon vanilla
1 cup chopped walnuts

1. Put the butter and chocolate in the top of a double boiler and place over hot water. Stir until melted. Remove from the heat and cool.
2. Sift the flour with the baking powder and salt. Set aside.
3. Beat the eggs until pale yellow.
4. Add the sugar and vanilla and heat until smooth.
5. Pour in the chocolate mixture and mix thoroughly.
6. Add the flour and walnuts. Blend well.
7. Pour into an 8-inch (20-cm) square pan lined with wax paper.
8. Bake in a 350°F (180°C) oven for about ½ hour. Cool and cut into squares.

Makes about 16.

Date Bars

3 eggs, beaten
1 cup sugar
1 cup all-purpose flour
¼ teaspoon salt
1 teaspoon baking powder

½ teaspoon cinnamon
1½ cups sliced dates
1¼ teaspoons vanilla
1 cup broken pecans
confectioners' sugar

1. Beat the eggs with the sugar until thick and creamy.
2. Sift the flour with the salt, baking powder and cinnamon. Add to the egg and sugar mixture and beat until smooth.
3. Add the dates, vanilla and pecans. Mix thoroughly.
4. Pour into an 8-inch x 12-inch (20-cm x 30-cm) pan lined with wax paper.
5. Bake in a 350°F (180°C) oven for about ½ hour. Cut into small bars while still warm and roll in confectioners' sugar.

Makes about 2 dozen.

Apricot Surprises

¼ lb (125 g) cream cheese	dried apricots
⅔ cup (165 g) butter	milk
⅔ cup sugar	sugar
1⅓ cups all-purpose flour	

1. Cream together the cream cheese, butter and sugar.
2. Add the flour and mix thoroughly.
3. Form into rolls about one inch (2½ cm) in diameter. Wrap in wax paper and chill for several hours.
4. Unwrap and cut into thin slices.
5. Place a piece of dried apricot on one slice and top with another. Press the edges together.
6. Brush each cookie with milk and sprinkle with sugar.
7. Place on a buttered cookie sheet and bake in a 350°F (180°C) oven for about seven minutes.

Makes about 3 dozen.

Chocolate Crispies

2 eggs	½ cup (125 g) butter
1 cup sugar	½ cup all-purpose flour
¾ teaspoon vanilla	½ cup chopped walnuts
2 oz (60 g) cooking chocolate	

1. Beat the eggs until pale yellow.
2. Add the sugar and vanilla and beat until thick and creamy.
3. Put the chocolate and butter in a small saucepan and melt over a low heat. Cool slightly and add to the egg and sugar mixture. Beat until smooth.
4. Add the flour and mix thoroughly.
5. Spread the mixture in an 8-inch (20-cm) square pan lined with wax paper.
6. Sprinkle on the nuts and bake in a 325°F (160°C) oven for about ½ hour. Cut into squares while warm and remove from the pan.

Makes about 2 dozen squares.

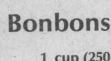

Bonbons

1 cup (250 g) butter	2½ cups all-purpose flour
1½ cups confectioners' sugar	1 teaspoon baking soda
1 egg, beaten	1 teaspoon baking powder
½ teaspoon vanilla	blanched almonds
½ teaspoon almond extract	

1. Cream together the butter and sugar until light and fluffy.
2. Add the egg, vanilla and almond extract and beat well.
3. Sift together the flour, baking soda and baking powder. Add to the creamed mixture and mix thoroughly.
4. Form into small balls and place on a buttered cookie sheet. Make a slight depression into each cookie and put in a blanched almond.
5. Bake in a 375°F (190°C) oven for about 15 minutes.

Makes about 5 dozen.

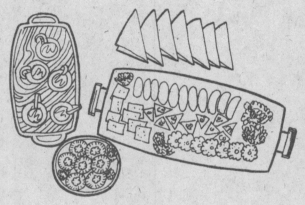

Gingersnaps

¾ cup (185 g) butter	¼ teaspoon salt
1 cup sugar	2 teaspoons baking soda
¼ cup (65 ml) molasses	¾ teaspoon cinnamon
1 egg, beaten	¾ teaspoon cloves
2 cups all-purpose flour	1½ teaspoons ginger

1. Cream together the butter and sugar until light and fluffy.
2. Add the molasses and egg and beat well.
3. Sift together the flour, salt, baking soda, cinnamon, cloves and ginger. Add to the creamed mixture and mix thoroughly.
4. Roll into small balls and dip into sugar.
5. Place the balls on a buttered cookie sheet about 2 inches (5 cm) apart. Bake in a 375°F (190°C) oven for about 15 minutes.

Makes about 4 dozen.

Peanut Butter Cookies

1 cup (250 g) butter
1 teaspoon vanilla
1 cup sugar
1 cup brown sugar
2 eggs, beaten

1 cup peanut butter
3 cups all-purpose flour
⅛ teaspoon salt
2 teaspoons baking soda

1. Cream together the butter, vanilla and sugars until light and fluffy.
2. Add the eggs and beat well.
3. Stir in the peanut butter.
4. Sift together the flour, salt and baking soda and add to the peanut butter mixture.
5. Shape into small balls and place on a buttered cookie sheet. Press each ball down with a fork.
6. Bake in a 375°F (190°C) oven for about ten minutes.

Makes about 5 dozen.

Pecan Sandies

1 cup (250 g) butter
¼ cup confectioners' sugar
2 teaspoons vanilla
1 tablespoon water
2 cups all-purpose flour
1 cup chopped pecans

1. Cream together the butter and sugar.
2. Add the vanilla and the water.
3. Sift the flour and add to the butter mixture.
4. Stir in the pecans.
5. Form into small logs about 1½ inches (4 cm) long.
6. Place on an ungreased cookie sheet and bake in a 300°F (150°C) oven for about 20 minutes or until lightly browned. While still hot, roll in confectioners' sugar.

Makes about 3 dozen.

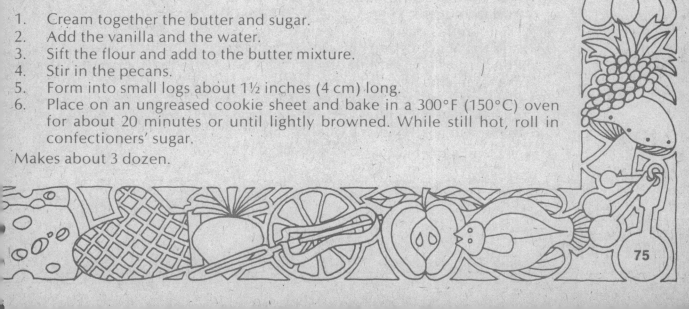

Carrington Cookies

3 cups all-purpose flour
2 teaspoons baking powder
1 teaspoon ground cloves
2 tablespoons cinnamon
½ teaspoon nutmeg

1 cup candied orange and lemon peel
1 tablespoon grated lemon rind
4 eggs
2 cups sugar

1. Sift together the flour, baking powder, cloves, cinnamon and nutmeg into a large mixing bowl.
2. Stir in the peel and grated lemon rind.
3. Beat the eggs with the sugar until thick and creamy.
4. Add the flour mixture and mix to a smooth dough.
5. Roll out on a floured board to a thickness of ¼ inch (5 mm).
6. Place on a buttered cookie sheet and bake in a 350°F (180°C) oven for about 15 minutes.

Makes about 4 dozen.

Zimmertstern

6 egg whites
3½ cups confectioners' sugar
1 teaspoon grated lemon rind
1 lb (500 g) ground almonds
1 teaspoon cinnamon

1. Beat the egg whites until stiff.
2. Add the sugar and lemon peel slowly while continuing to beat. Reserve ⅓ cup of this mixture to use on the top of the cookies.
3. Add the almonds and cinnamon and mix well. Chill for several hours.
4. Roll out on a board to a thickness of ¼ inch (5 mm). Spread a little of the reserved egg white on each one.
5. Place on wax paper on a cookie sheet and bake in a 325°F (160°C) oven for about ten minutes or until light brown. Remove from wax paper immediately after taking out of the oven.

Makes about 4 dozen.

Swedish Cookies

1½ cups (375 g) butter
1 cup sugar
1 egg, beaten
1 teaspoon vanilla
4 cups all-purpose flour
1 teaspoon baking powder

1. Cream together the butter and sugar until light and fluffy.
2. Add the egg and vanilla and beat well.
3. Sift together the flour and baking powder and mix to a smooth dough.
4. Shape into small balls and press down gently, or force through a cookie press into different shapes.
5. Put onto a lightly buttered cookie sheet and bake in 400°F (200°C) oven for about ten minutes.

Makes about 4 dozen.

Honey Cakes

2 eggs
1 cup sugar
⅓ cup honey
¾ cup slivered almonds
2½ cups all-purpose flour
¼ teaspoon baking soda

½ teaspoon cinnamon
¼ teaspoon nutmeg
½ teaspoon cloves
⅔ cup chopped orange peel
2 tablespoons chopped lemon peel

1. Beat together the eggs and sugar until thick and creamy.
2. Add the honey and mix well.
3. Stir in the slivered almonds.
4. Sift together the flour, baking soda, cinnamon, nutmeg and cloves. Add to the almond mixture.
5. Add the orange and lemon peel and mix thoroughly. Chill for several hours.
6. Roll the dough out on a floured board to a thickness of ½ inch (one cm). Cut with a round cookie cutter and place on a buttered cookie sheet.
7. Bake in a 350°F (180°C) oven for about 20 minutes.

Makes about 3 dozen.

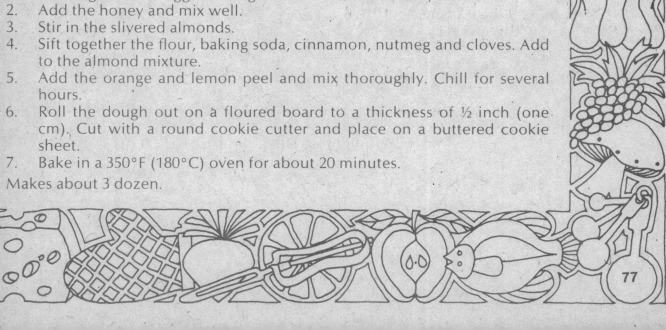

Date-Nut Fingers

¼ teaspoon salt
3 egg whites
1¾ cups confectioners' sugar
1 tablespoon all-purpose flour

2 cups coarsely chopped walnuts
1 cup chopped dates
1 teaspoon vanilla

1. Add salt to the egg whites and beat until frothy.
2. Add the sugar mixed with the flour one tablespoon at a time while continuing to beat until stiff.
3. Fold in the nuts, dates and vanilla.
4. Drop by the spoonful onto a cookie sheet covered with wax paper. Shape into finger.
5. Bake in a 300°F (150°C) oven for ½ hour. Remove from the paper immediately after taking out of the oven.

Makes about 2 dozen.

Chocolate Drops

1 lb (500 g) milk chocolate
2 oz (60 g) cooking chocolate
1 cup chopped nuts
1 cup chopped raisins
¼ teaspoon salt
5 cups corn flakes

1. Melt both the chocolates in the top of a double boiler over hot water.
2. Mix together the nuts, raisins, salt and corn flakes. Add to the chocolate and mix thoroughly.
3. Drop by the spoonful onto greaseproof paper. Chill for about one hour or until firm.

Makes about 3 dozen.

Coconut Macaroons

2 cups moist, shredded coconut
½ cup (125 g) sweetened
   condensed milk
1 teaspoon vanilla

1. Mix together the coconut and milk.
2. Add the vanilla and mix well.
3. Drop by the spoonful onto a buttered cookie sheet about one inch (2½ cm) apart.
4. Bake in a 350°F (180°C) oven for about ten minutes or until golden brown. Remove from the sheet immediately or they will stick. If they do stick, return to the oven and heat through.

Makes about 2 dozen.

Coconut Drops

2 egg whites
1 cup brown sugar
2 cups corn flakes
½ cup chopped walnuts

1 cup moist shredded coconut
½ teaspoon vanilla
sugar

1. Beat the egg whites until stiff.
2. Add the sugar while continuing to beat.
3. Fold in the corn flakes, walnuts and coconut.
4. Add the vanilla and mix well.
5. Drop by the spoonful onto a buttered cookie sheet.
6. Bake in a 350°F (180°C) oven for about 15 minutes.
7. When you remove the cookie sheets from the oven, put onto damp tea towels. Remove the cookies immediately. (If they stick to the sheet, return to the oven and heat through).
8. Sprinkle right away with sugar.

Makes about 1½ dozen.

Mincemeat Drop Cookies

¾ cup (185 g) butter
1½ cups sugar
3 eggs, beaten
3 cups all-purpose flour
¾ teaspoon salt

1 teaspoon baking soda
9 oz (280 g) mincemeat
2½ tablespoons water
1 cup chopped walnuts

1. Cream together the butter and sugar until light and fluffy.
2. Add the eggs and beat well.
3. Sift together the flour, salt and baking soda. Add half the sifted mixture to the creamed mixture.
4. Add the mincemeat and water and blend thoroughly.
5. Add the nuts and the rest of the flour mixture. Mix well.
6. Drop by the spoonful onto a buttered cookie sheet.
7. Bake in a 350°F (180°C) oven for about ten minutes.

Makes about 4 dozen.

Ice Cream Cookies

½ cup (125 g) butter
1 cup confectioners' sugar
1 egg yolk, beaten
1 teaspoon vanilla
1 cup all-purpose flour
glacé cherries

1. Cream together the butter and sugar until light and fluffy.
2. Add the egg yolk and vanilla and beat well.
3. Sift the flour and add to the creamed mixture.
4. Drop by the spoonful onto a buttered cookie sheet.
5. Top with glacé cherries and bake in a 350°F (180°C) oven for about 15 minutes.

Makes about 2 dozen.

Orange Drop Cookies

1 cup (250 g) butter
1½ cups brown sugar
2 eggs, beaten
¼ cup (65 ml) orange juice
3 teaspoons grated orange rind
1 teaspoon grated lemon rind
1 teaspoon vanilla

1 cup (250 ml) sour milk*
3½ cups all-purpose flour
¼ teaspoon salt
2 teaspoons baking powder
1 teaspoon baking soda
½ cup chopped nuts
½ cup chopped dates

1. Cream together the butter and sugar until light and fluffy.
2. Add the eggs, orange juice, grated orange and lemon peel, vanilla and sour milk and beat thoroughly.
3. Sift together the flour, salt, baking powder and baking soda. Add to the beaten mixture.
4. Add the nuts and dates and mix well.
5. Drop by the spoonful onto a buttered cookie sheet.
6. Bake in a 350°F (180°C) oven for about 15 minutes.

Makes about 5 dozen.

* (To sour milk, mix in a teaspoon of vinegar and set aside for ten minutes.)

Hermit Cookies

1 cup (250 g) butter
2 cups brown sugar
2 eggs, beaten
3½ cups all-purpose flour
½ teaspoon salt
1 teaspoon baking powder
1 teaspoon baking soda

1½ teaspoons cinnamon
1½ teaspoons nutmeg
½ cup (125 ml) sour milk*
1 cup raisins
1 cup chopped dates
1 cup chopped walnuts

1. Cream together the butter and sugar until light and fluffy.
2. Add the eggs and beat well.
3. Sift together the flour, salt, baking powder, baking soda, cinnamon and nutmeg. Add to the creamed mixture alternately with the sour milk.
4. Mix in the raisins, dates and walnuts.
5. Drop by the spoonful onto a buttered cookie sheet.
6. Bake in a 375°F (190°C) oven for about 15 minutes.

Makes about 4 dozen.

* (To sour the milk, mix in a teaspoon of vinegar or lemon juice and allow to stand for ten minutes.)

81

Drop Sugar Cookies

½ cup (125 g) butter
¾ cup sugar
1 egg
½ teaspoon vanilla
½ teaspoon grated orange rind
1½ cups all-purpose flour
¼ teaspoon salt

½ teaspoon baking powder
2½ tablespoons milk
1 cup raisins
½ cup candied orange and lemon peel
glacé cherries

1. Cream together the butter and sugar until light and fluffy.
2. Add the eggs and beat well.
3. Stir in the vanilla and orange rind.
4. Sift together the flour, salt and baking powder and add alternately with the milk.
5. Add the raisins and peel and stir until well blended.
6. Drop by the spoonful onto a buttered cookie sheet.
7. Top with a glacé cherry and bake in a 375°F (190°C) oven for about 12 minutes.

Makes about 4 dozen.

Chocolate Drop Cookies

½ cup (125 g) butter
1 cup brown sugar
1 egg, beaten
1 teaspoon vanilla
2 oz (60 g) cooking chocolate, melted

1⅔ cups all-purpose flour
½ teaspoon salt
½ teaspoon baking soda
½ cup (125 ml) milk
½ cup chopped walnuts

1. Cream together the butter and sugar until light and fluffy.
2. Add the egg, vanilla and chocolate and blend thoroughly.
3. Sift together the flour, salt and baking soda and stir into the chocolate mixture.
4. Add the milk and walnuts and mix well.
5. Drop by the spoonful onto a buttered cookie sheet.
6. Bake in a 350°F (180°C) oven for about ten minutes.

Makes about 2 dozen.

Florentines

⅓ cup (85 g) unsalted butter
½ cup sugar
¼ cup chopped glacé cherries
1 cup chopped blanched almonds

¼ cup slivered almonds
½ cup candied orange and lemon peel
3 tablespoons cream
¼ lb (125 g) grated milk chocolate

1. Melt the butter in a saucepan over low heat.
2. Add the sugar and bring to the boil.
3. Add the cherries, chopped and slivered almonds, and peel. Cook until well combined.
4. Remove the saucepan from the heat and stir in the cream. Cool.
5. When the mixture is cold, drop by the spoonful onto a baking sheet lined with buttered and floured wax paper. Leave enough room around each one to allow for spreading during the cooking.
6. Bake in a 350°F (180°C) oven for about 15 minutes. Remove from the oven and set aside.
7. Heat the chocolate until it has melted.
8. When the florentines are firm, remove from the wax paper.
9. Spread with the chocolate as the chocolate begins to set. Leave until completely set.

Cream Cheese Cookies

½ cup (125 g) butter
½ cup sugar
¼ lb (125 g) cream cheese
1 egg, beaten

2 cups all-purpose flour
¼ teaspoon salt
1 teaspoon baking powder

1. Cream together the butter and sugar until light and fluffy.
2. Add the softened cream cheese and half the egg. Beat thoroughly.
3. Sift together the flour, salt and baking powder and add to the cream cheese mixture. Blend thoroughly.
4. Shape into rolls about 1½ inches (4 cm) in diameter and wrap in wax paper. Chill for several hours.
5. Cut into thin slices and put onto a greased cookie sheet.
6. Brush the cookies with the rest of the egg and allow to dry.
7. Bake in a 350°F (180°C) oven for ten minutes.

Makes about 5 dozen.

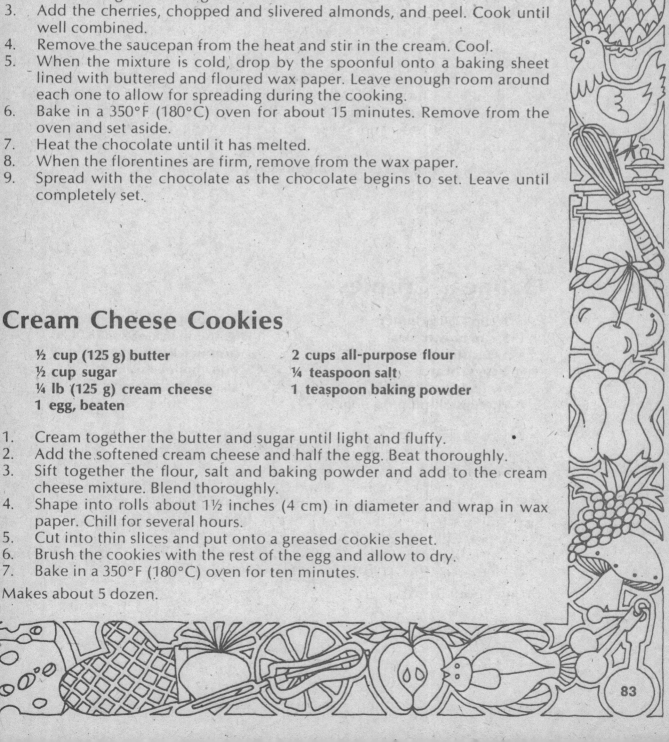

Old-Fashioned Sugar Cookies

½ cup (125 g) butter	2 cups all-purpose flour
¾ cup sugar	¼ teaspoon salt
1 egg	¾ teaspoon baking powder
½ teaspoon vanilla	2½ tablespoons milk
½ teaspoon grated orange rind	sugar

1. Cream together the butter and sugar until light and fluffy.
2. Add the egg and beat well.
3. Stir in the vanilla and orange rind.
4. Sift together the flour, salt and baking powder and add alternately with the milk. Mix to a dough.
5. Roll out on a floured board to a thickness of ¼ inch (5 mm) and cut with a cookie cutter in the shapes desired.
6. Sprinkle with sugar and place on a lightly buttered cookie sheet. Bake in a 375°F (190°C) oven for about 12 minutes or until golden brown. Cool slightly on the sheet before removing to a wire rack to cool completely.

Makes about 3 dozen (depending on size).

Oatmeal Crispies

1 cup (250 g) butter	1 teaspoon salt
1 cup brown sugar	1 teaspoon baking soda
1 cup sugar	3 cups quick-cooking oatmeal
2 eggs, beaten	½ cup chopped walnuts
1¼ teaspoons vanilla	½ teaspoon cinnamon
1½ cups all-purpose flour	

1. Cream together the butter and sugars until light and fluffy.
2. Add the eggs and vanilla and beat well.
3. Sift together the flour, salt and baking soda and add to the mixture.
4. Stir in the oatmeal, walnuts and cinnamon and mix well.
5. Shape into rolls about 2 inches (5 cm) in diameter and wrap in wax paper. Chill for several hours.
6. Cut into slices ¼ inch (5 mm) thick and bake on an ungreased cookie sheet in a 350°F (180°C) oven for about ten minutes.

Makes about 5 dozen.

Lemon-Pecan Dainties

½ cup (125 g) butter
1 cup sugar
1 egg, beaten
1 tablespoon lemon juice
3 teaspoons grated lemon rind

2 cups all-purpose flour
⅛ teaspoon salt
1 teaspoon baking powder
1 cup chopped pecans

1. Cream together the butter and sugar until light and fluffy.
2. Add the egg, lemon juice and lemon rind and beat well.
3. Sift together the flour, salt and baking powder and add to the lemon mixture.
4. Stir in the nuts.
5. Shape into rolls about 1½ inches (4 cm) in diameter. Wrap in wax paper and chill for several hours.
6. Cut into thin slices and place on a greased cookie sheet.
7. Bake in a 350°F (180°C) oven for about 12 minutes.

Makes about 5 dozen.

Refrigerator Cookies

½ cup (125 g) butter
½ cup brown sugar
¾ cup sugar
1 egg
1¼ teaspoons vanilla

½ cup chopped walnuts
2 cups all-purpose flour
½ teaspoon salt
2 teaspoons baking powder

1. Cream together the butter and sugars until light and fluffy.
2. Add the egg and beat well.
3. Add the vanilla and nuts.
4. Sift together the flour, salt and baking powder and mix into the butter and sugar mixture.
5. Shape into rolls 1½ inches (4 cm) in diameter. Roll in wax paper. Chill for several hours.
6. Cut into thin slices and bake on a greased cookie sheet in a 425°F (220°C) oven for ten minutes.

Makes about 4 dozen.

Date-Filled Cookies

½ cup (125 g) butter
2 cups brown sugar
2 eggs, beaten
1 teaspoon vanilla
3½ cups all-purpose flour
½ teaspoon salt
1 teaspoon baking soda
1 teaspoon baking powder

Date Filling:
1 lb (500 g) dates, chopped
½ cup brown sugar
½ cup (125 ml) water
½ cup chopped walnuts

1. Cream together the butter and sugar until light and fluffy.
2. Add the eggs and vanilla and beat well.
3. Sift together the flour, salt, baking soda and baking powder. Mix into the butter and sugar mixture.
4. Shape into rolls about 1½ inches (4 cm) in diameter. Wrap in wax paper and chill for several hours.
5. Meanwhile make the Date Filling by mixing together the dates, sugar and water in a saucepan. Bring to the boil. Reduce heat and simmer until thick. Remove from heat and cool. Stir in the walnuts.
6. Cut the cookie dough into thin slices. Place a teaspoon of the filling on half the slices. Top with the rest of the slices. Press edges together with a fork.
7. Place on a buttered cookie sheet and bake in 350°F (180°C) oven for about ten minutes.

Makes about 4 dozen.

Scotch Shortbread

1 cup (250 g) butter
1 cup sugar
3 cups all-purpose flour

1. Cream together the butter and sugar.
2. Add 2½ cups of flour and mix thoroughly.
3. Sprinkle the remaining ½ cup of flour on a board and knead until the dough cracks.
4. Roll out to a thickness of ¼ inch (5 mm). Cut into desired shapes.
5. Place on an ungreased cookie sheet and bake in a 275°F (140°C) oven for 50 minutes or until golden.

Makes about 2 dozen.

Chocolate Refrigerator Cookies

½ cup (125 g) butter
1 cup brown sugar
1 egg
2 oz (60 g) cooking chocolate, melted
¾ teaspoon vanilla

½ cup chopped walnuts
2 cups all-purpose flour
¼ teaspoon salt
¾ teaspoon baking powder
¼ teaspoon baking soda
2½ tablespoons milk

1. Cream together the butter and sugar until light and fluffy.
2. Add the egg and beat well.
3. Add the chocolate and vanilla and mix thoroughly.
4. Stir in the nuts.
5. Sift together the flour, salt, baking powder and baking soda and add to the chocolate mixture alternately with the milk. Mix well.
6. Shape into rolls 1½ inches (4 cm) in diameter. Roll in wax paper and chill for several hours.
7. Cut into thin slices and place on a greased cookie sheet.
8. Bake in a 400°F (200°C) oven for about ten minutes.

Makes 4 dozen.

Pinwheel Cookies

½ cup (125 g) butter
½ cup sugar
1 egg yolk
1½ teaspoons vanilla
1½ cups all-purpose flour

¼ teaspoon salt
½ teaspoon baking powder
2½ tablespoons milk
1 oz (30 g) cooking chocolate, melted

1. Cream together the butter and sugar until light and fluffy.
2. Add the egg yolk and vanilla essence and mix well.
3. Sift together the flour, salt and baking powder and add alternately with the milk.
4. Divide the dough in half and add the chocolate to one half.
5. Roll each half out to a thickness of ⅛ inch (3 mm) on a floured board. Put the white part on top of the chocolate and roll up. Wrap in wax paper and chill for several hours.
6. Cut into thin slices and put on an ungreased cookie sheet. Bake in a 375°F (190°C) oven for about ten minutes.

Makes 4 dozen.

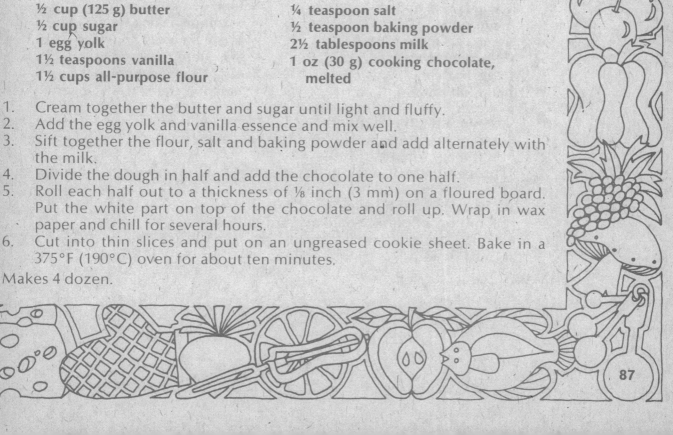

Vanilla Wafers

1 cup (250 g) butter
1½ cups sugar
3 eggs
3 cups all-purpose flour

3 teaspoons baking powder
1 tablespoon milk
2 teaspoons vanilla

1. Cream together the butter and sugar until light and fluffy.
2. Add the eggs one at a time beating well after each addition.
3. Sift together the flour and baking powder and mix into the creamed mixture.
4. Blend the milk and vanilla and add to the mixture. Mix thoroughly. Chill for about an hour.
5. Roll out on a floured board to a thickness of ¼ inch (5 mm).
6. Cut into shapes desired and place on a buttered cookie sheet.
7. Bake in a 400°F (200°C) oven for about seven minutes or until golden brown.

Makes about 4 dozen.

Ginger Cookies

½ cup (125 g) butter
½ cup sugar
½ cup (125 ml) molasses
1½ teaspoons vinegar
1 egg, beaten
3 cups all-purpose flour

¼ teaspoon salt
½ teaspoon baking soda
½ teaspoon baking powder
½ teaspoon cinnamon
½ teaspoon ginger powder
1 teaspoon grated fresh ginger

1. Mix together the butter, sugar, molasses and vinegar in a saucepan. Bring to the boil. Remove from the heat and cool.
2. Add the egg and beat well.
3. Sift together the flour, salt, baking soda, baking powder, cinnamon, and ginger powder. Add to the mixture and beat well.
4. Stir in the grated fresh ginger. Chill for one hour.
5. Roll out on a floured board and cut into shapes.
6. Put on a buttered cookie sheet and bake in a 375°F (190°C) oven for about 15 minutes.

Makes about 2 dozen.

Fig Bars

½ cup (125 g) butter
¾ cup sugar
1 egg
½ teaspoon vanilla
½ teaspoon grated orange rind
2 cups all-purpose flour
¼ teaspoon salt
¼ teaspoon cinnamon
¾ teaspoon baking powder
2½ tablespoons milk

Filling:
1 cup chopped figs
2 teaspoons grated lemon rind
1 cup (250 ml) boiling water
½ cup sugar
2 tablespoons all-purpose flour
¼ teaspoon nutmeg

1. Cream together the butter and sugar until light and fluffy.
2. Add the egg and beat well.
3. Stir in the vanilla and orange rind.
4. Sift the flour with the salt and baking powder and add alternately with the milk. Mix to a dough.
5. Roll out on a floured board to a thickness of ¼ inch (5 mm). Cut into long strips 3 inches (8 cm) wide. Set aside.
6. Mix together the figs, lemon rind and boiling water in a saucepan.
7. Add the sugar, flour, nutmeg and cinnamon. Beat well.
8. Cook over a medium heat, stirring frequently, for five minutes. Cool.
9. Spread half the strips with the filling. Cover with the remaining strips. Press the edges together with a fork. Cut into 2-inch (5-cm) lengths.
10. Place on a buttered cookie sheet and cook in a 350°F (180°C) oven for about 20 minutes.

Makes about 18 bars.

Georgia Cream Cookies

1 cup (250 g) butter	1 teaspoon salt
2 cups sugar	3 teaspoons baking powder
3 eggs, beaten	½ teaspoon baking soda
1 teaspoon vanilla	1½ cups chopped walnuts
1 cup (250 g) sour cream	3 tablespoons sugar
5 cups all-purpose flour	1 teaspoon cinnamon

1. Cream together the butter and sugar until light and fluffy.
2. Add the eggs, vanilla and sour cream and beat well.
3. Sift together the flour, salt, baking powder and baking soda. Stir into the beaten mixture.
4. Add the walnuts and blend thoroughly.
5. Drop by the spoonful onto a buttered cookie sheet.
6. Mix together the sugar and cinnamon.
7. Butter the bottom of a small glass and dip into the sugar-cinnamon mixture. Press the cookies flat.
8. Bake in a 350°F (180°C) oven for about 15 minutes.

Makes about 6 dozen.

Molasses Cookies

¾ cup (185 g) butter	1 teaspoon salt
1 cup sugar	1 teaspoon baking soda
2 eggs, beaten	1½ teaspoons cinnamon
1 cup molasses	1½ teaspoons ginger
4 cups all-purpose flour	¾ cup (185 ml) strong coffee

1. Cream together the butter and sugar until light and fluffy.
2. Add the eggs and molasses and beat well.
3. Sift together the flour, salt, baking soda, cinnamon and ginger and mix into the molasses mixture alternately with the cold coffee.
4. Drop by the teaspoon onto a buttered cookie sheet.
5. Bake in a 350°F (180°C) oven for about 15 minutes.

Makes about 6 dozen.

Chocolate Chip Cookies

½ cup (125 g) butter
1 teaspoon vanilla
½ cup sugar
¼ cup brown sugar
1 egg, beaten

1½ cups all-purpose flour
½ teaspoon salt
½ teaspoon baking soda
½ lb (250 g) choc-bits
½ cup chopped walnuts

1. Cream together the butter, vanilla and sugars until light and fluffy.
2. Add the egg and beat well.
3. Sift together the flour, salt and baking soda and add to the creamed mixture.
4. Add the choc-bits and walnuts and mix thoroughly.
5. Drop by the spoonful onto a buttered cookie sheet.
6. Bake in a 350°F (190°C) oven for about 12 minutes.

Makes about 4 dozen.

Pecan Cookies

½ cup (125 g) butter
½ cup sugar
2½ cups brown sugar
2 eggs, beaten

2½ cups all-purpose flour
¼ teaspoon salt
½ teaspoon baking soda
1 cup chopped pecans

1. Cream together the butter and sugars until light and fluffy.
2. Add the eggs and beat well.
3. Sift together the flour, salt and baking soda and add to the creamed mixture.
4. Stir in the nuts.
5. Drop by the spoonful onto a buttered cookie sheet. Leave about 2 inches (5 cm) between the cookies as they will spread.
6. Bake in a 350°F (180°C) oven for about 12 minutes.

Makes about 5 dozen.

Fairy Cookies

¼ cup (65 g) butter	¼ cup raspberry jam
¼ cup sugar	2 teaspoon lemon juice
¾ cup all-purpose flour	
¼ cup cornstarch	Meringue:
3 teaspoons cold water	2 egg whites
¾ teaspoon vanilla	½ cup sugar

1. Cream the butter with the sugar until light and fluffy.
2. Sift together the flour and cornstarch and add to the creamed mixture.
3. Add the water and vanilla. Knead the dough for one minute.
4. Roll out on a floured board to a thickness of ¼ inch (5 mm). Cut into 1½-inch (4-cm) circles and put on a buttered baking sheet. Bake in a 350°F (180°C) oven for 8-10 minutes.
5. Blend the jam with the lemon juice and put a spoonful into the center of each cookie.
6. Beat the egg whites until stiff. Add the sugar and continue beating for another minute.
7. Spoon the egg white mixture over the cookies ensuring that the cooki is completely covered. Bake for another 8-10 minutes. Allow to coo slightly on the baking sheet before transferring to a wire rack to coo completely.

Makes 12-15.

Butterscotch Squares

½ cup (125 g) butter	¼ teaspoon salt
2 cups brown sugar	2 teaspoons baking powder
2 eggs	1 cup flaked coconut
1¼ teaspoons vanilla	½ cup chopped walnuts
2 cups all-purpose flour	

1. Mix the butter and sugar in a saucepan and cook over a low heat stirring constantly, until bubbly. Remove from the heat and cool.
2. Add the eggs one at a time beating well after each addition.
3. Stir in the vanilla.
4. Sift together the flour, salt and baking powder and add to th butterscotch mixture.
5. Stir in the coconut and nuts.
6. Spread in a 10-inch x 14-inch (25-cm x 35-cm) buttered and floure pan.
7. Bake in a 350°F (180°C) oven for about 25 minutes. Cut into square while still warm. Makes about 3 dozen.

Mixed Fruit Drop Cookies

¾ cup (185 g) butter
1½ cups sugar
3 eggs, beaten
3 cups all-purpose flour
1 teaspoon salt

1 teaspoon baking soda
½ lb (250 g) mixed dried fruit
3 tablespoons water
1 cup chopped nuts

1. Cream together the butter and sugar until light and fluffy.
2. Add the eggs and mix well.
3. Sift together the flour, salt and baking soda and add half to the creamed mixture.
4. Add the mixed fruit and water and blend thoroughly.
5. Mix in the nuts and the remaining flour and mix well. (If the mixture is too dry, add a little more water.)
6. Drop from a teaspoon onto a greased cookie sheet.
7. Bake in a 350°F (180°C) oven for about ten minutes.

Makes about 4 dozen.

Sugar Nut Strips

½ cup (125 g) unsalted butter
⅓ cup sugar
1 egg
1 cup all-purpose flour, sifted

¼ teaspoon salt
1 egg yolk
1 teaspoon water
½ cup finely ground nuts

1. Cream together the butter and sugar until light and fluffy.
2. Add the egg and mix well.
3. Add the flour and salt and mix to a smooth dough. Chill in the refrigerator for at least ½ hour.
4. Roll out on a floured board to a thickness of ⅛ inch (3 mm). Trim the edges and place on a cookie sheet uncut.
5. Beat the egg yolk with the water and brush on the dough.
6. Sprinkle with the nuts.
7. Bake in a 350°F (180°C) oven for about 15 minutes. Cut into 1 inch x 2 inch (2½ cm x 5 cm) strips before completely cool.

Hazelnut Creams

1 cup (250 g) butter	2 cups cake flour
½ cup sugar	raspberry jam
½ lb (250 g) finely ground hazelnuts	Lemon Cream

1. Cream together the butter and sugar until light and fluffy.
2. Add the hazelnuts and flour and mix until the dough is smooth. Put into the refrigerator and chill for at least ½ hour.
3. Roll out the dough to a thickness of ⅛ inch (3 mm) on a floured board or between two pieces of wax paper. Cut into small rounds.
4. Bake on an ungreased cookie sheet in a 350°F (180°C) oven for ten to fifteen minutes. Cool.
5. Spread raspberry jam on one cookie and Lemon Cream on the other and sandwich together.

Makes about 3 dozen depending on the size.

Lemon Cream

Mix one cup of confectioners' sugar with one tablespoon of lemon juice and one tablespoon of butter.

Teacakes

2 cups all-purpose flour	3 tablespoons milk
2 teaspoons baking powder	½ cup chopped candied orange
pinch of salt	and lemon peel
½ cup (125 g) butter	½ cup currants
½ cup sugar	1 egg white
1 egg	sugar

1. Sift together the flour, baking powder and salt.
2. Combine the butter, sugar and egg. Mix until smooth and creamy.
3. Add the milk, peel and currants to the butter mixture.
4. Stir in the sifted dry ingredients. Mix well and put into the refrigerator to chill for about ½ hour.
5. Shape the dough into small balls about the size of walnuts. Dip the tops in the slightly beaten egg white, then the sugar. Place on a greased cookie sheet, sugar side up.
6. Bake in a 400°F (200°C) oven for about 15 minutes.

Index

Almond Cakes 25
Almond Coconut Bars 70
Almond Crescents 16
Almond Stars 57
Apricot Cookies 34
Apricot-Nut Delights 35
Apricot Surprises 73

Banana Oatmeal Cookies 16
Bird's Nest Cookies 9
Black Eye Susans 45
Bonbons 74
Brandy Snaps 38
Brazil Nut Bars 64
Brazil Nut Cookies 49
Brownies 72
Butter Almond Cookies 10
Butterscotch Cookies 45
Butterscotch-Pecan Cookies 29
Butterscotch Squares 92
Butter Wafers 55

Carrington Cookies 76
Cheesy Lemon Cookies 49
Cherry-Coconut Drops 54
Choc-Almond Cookies 33
Choc-Logs 39
Chocolate Chip Cookies 91
Chocolate Cream Sandwiches 43
Chocolate Crispies 73
Chocolate Date Cookies 32
Chocolate Diamonds 62
Chocolate Drop Cookies 82
Chocolate Drops 78
Chocolate Macaroons 31
Chocolate Nut Shortbread 11
Chocolate Refrigerator Cookies 87
Chocolate Walnuts 43
Choc Tops 59
Christmas Cookies 17

Cinnamon Curls 41
Cinnamon Squares 41
Clover Leaf Cookies 42
Coconut Chews 36
Coconut Drops 79
Coconut Kisses 54
Coconut Macaroons 79
Coconut-Nut Bars 68
Coconut Rings 60
Coconut Squares 64
Corn Meal Wafers 20
Cream Cheese Cookies 83
Crispie-Coconut Squares 70
Crispy Ginger Cookies 61

Date Bars 72
Date-Filled Cookies 86
Date Kisses 19
Date-Nut Fingers 78
Date-Nut Swirls 28
Date Roll-Ups 44
Digestive Cookies 13
Drop Sugar Cookies 82

Egg Shortbread 58
Egg White Wafers 30

Fairy Cookies 92
Fig Bars 89
Fig Cakes 25
Finnish Cookies 19
Florentines 83
Fruity Drops 52
Fruity Oatmeal Cookies 26
Fudgy Wafers 51

Georgia Cream Cookies 90
Ginger Cookies 88
Gingernuts 39
Gingersnaps 74
Ginger Sugar Squares 66
Glazed Almond Cookies 46

WAYS TO PREPARE BISCUITS AND COOKIES

Golden Cookies 57
Golden Fries 31
Gold Nuggets 47
Grandma's Sugar Cookies 23

Hazelnut Creams 94
Hermit Cookies 81
Hermits 55
Honey Cakes 77
Honey-Date Squares 65
Honey-Spice Cookies 14

Iced Chocolate Circles 34
Ice Cream Cookies 80
Iced Ginger Cookies 42
Island Cookies 15

Jam Sandwich Cookies 59

Lace Cookies 28
Lebkuchen 20
Lemon Fingers 37
Lemon-Pecan Dainties 85
Lemon Shortbread Cookies 11
Lemon Wafers 12

Macadamian Balls 24
Marble Brownies 67
Marshmallow Creams 40
Melting Moments 37
Meringue Toppers 38
Mincemeat Drop Cookies 80
Mincemeat Hermits 52
Mincemeat Squares 63
Mixed Fruit Drop Cookies 93
Mocha Cookies 36
Molasses Cookies 90
Molasses Creams 68
Mother's Special Cookies 17

New Orleans Pecan Balls 24
Nut Ball Cookies 10
Nutmeg Butterballs 18
Nut Rocks 40
Nut Shortbread 58
Nutty Date Chews 63

Oatmeal Cookies 48
Oatmeal Crispies 84
Oatmeal-Date Bars 71
Oatmeal Drops 53
Oatmeal Rounds 30
Oatmeal Sandwiches 56
Oat-Peanut Cookies 51
Old-Fashioned Sugar Cookies 84
Orange Cookies 33
Orange Drop Cookies 81
Orange-Molasses Cookies 61
Orange Squares 69

Orange Thins 13

Peanut Butter Cookies 75
Peanut Butter Logs 46
Pecan Cookies 91
Pecan Dainties 48
Pecan Sandies 75
Pfeffernuesse 29
Pineapple Cookies 26
Pine-Nut Drops 53
Pinwheel Cookies 87
Prune Cookies 44

Raisin Sandwich Cookies 27
Refrigerator Cookies 85
Rice Shortbread 18
Rock Cakes 15
Rum Balls 47

Saucepan Brownies 66
Scandinavian Christmas Cookies 23
Scotch Shortbread 86
Seed Cookies 63
Sesame Seed Drops 50
Sherry Balls 21
Sour Cream Cookies 22
Spicy Drop Cookies 50
Spicy Walnut Squares 65
Sugar Bars 71
Sugar Nut Strips 93
Sugar Rings 60
Strawberry Cookies 14
Swedish Cookies 77
Sweet Sherry Cookies 56

Teacakes 94
Tom Thumbs 22

Vanilla Nuts 32
Vanilla Wafers 88
Victorian Tarts 21

Walnut Balls 27
Walnut Cookies 35
Walnut Crispies 12

Zimmertstern 76